GMDSS
A User's Handbook

Other titles of interest

Reeds VHF/DSC Handbook 3rd edition

Sue Fletcher ISBN 978-1-4081-3143-5

A user-friendly guide covering both the analogue and digital functions of the radio. The standard work on the subject, it contains all the information required to pass the Short Range Certificate and gives a full explanation of GMDSS.

Heavy Weather Sailing

Peter Bruce ISBN 978-1-4729-2319-6

The ultimate international authority on surviving storms at sea aboard sailing and motor vessels, thoroughly revised over 50 years in print to ensure it remains essential.

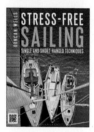

Stress-Free Sailing

Duncan Wells ISBN 978-1-4729-0743-1

This indispensable guide takes the stress out of sailing with step-by-step photographic instructions on how to perform essential sailing techniques, regardless of how much help you have to hand.

First Aid at Sea

Colin Berry & Douglas Justins ISBN 978-1-4081-5703-9

An easy-to-access instant guide to emergency first aid for all seafarers, including a colour-coded thumb index of emergencies for quick reference.

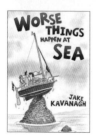

Worse Things Happen at Sea

Jake Kavanagh ISBN 978-1-4081-1642-5

Incorrect use of radio equipment is just one of the many hilarious tales in this humorous look at mishaps at sea. Illustrated with cartoons throughout, this is an admirable antidote to the serious side of boating.

6th EDITION

GMDSS
A User's Handbook

Denise Bréhaut

ADLARD COLES NAUTICAL

BLOOMSBURY

LONDON · OXFORD · NEW YORK · NEW DELHI · SYDNEY

For Jake, my friend, my hero and my safe haven.

Adlard Coles Nautical
An imprint of Bloomsbury Publishing Plc

50 Bedford Square
London
WC1B 3DP
UK

29 Earlsfort Terrace
Dublin 2
Ireland

1385 Broadway
New York
NY 10018
USA

www.bloomsbury.com
www.adlardcoles.com

ADLARD COLES, ADLARD COLES NAUTICAL and the Buoy logo are trademarks
of Bloomsbury Publishing Plc

First published 1999
Second edition 2002
Third edition 2006
Fourth edition 2009
Fifth edition 2013
Sixth edition 2017

British Library Cataloguing-in-Publication Data
A catalogue record for this book is available from the British Library.

Library of Congress Cataloguing-in-Publication data has been applied for.

ISBN: PB: 978-1-4729-4568-6
ePDF: 978-1-4729-4566-2
ePub: 978-1-4729-4567-9

6 8 10 9 7 5

Typeset in 9 on 12pt ITC Cheltenham Book by Susan McIntyre
Printed and bound in India by Replika Press Pvt. Ltd.

MIX
Paper from
responsible sources
FSC® C016779

To find out more about our authors and books visit www.bloomsbury.com. Here you will find extracts,
author interviews, details of forthcoming events and the option to sign up for our newsletters.

Contents

PREFACE   8

GLOSSARY OF ABBREVIATIONS   9

ACKNOWLEDGEMENTS   10

1 INTRODUCTION TO THE SYSTEMS **11**
Sea areas   13
Equipment requirements for compulsorily fitted vessels   14
Voluntarily fitted vessels   15
Questions   15
Answers   16

2 TRAINING COURSES AND EXAMINATIONS **17**
The General Operator's Certificate Course (GOC)   17
The GOC examination   17
The Long Range Certificate Course (LRC)   18
The LRC examination   18
Satellite module   19
The Restricted Operator's Certificate Course (ROC)   19
The ROC examination   19

3 MODES OF EMISSION AND PROPAGATION **20**
Modes of emission   20
Propagation of the radio wave   23
Types of radio waves   25
Practical uses within radio frequency bands   28
Questions   29
Answers   30

4 GENERAL REGULATIONS AND PROCEDURES **31**
Identification of stations   31
Radio watch   32
DSC watch keeping   33
Test transmissions   34
Documents   34
Transmissions in UK harbours   35
Simplex and duplex   35
The use of channels and frequencies in the maritime band   36
Transceiver functions   38
Maximum permitted transmitter power   39
The phonetic alphabet   39
Control of communications   40
Making a routine call   40
Difficulty with communications   41
Questions   41
Answers   43

5 DIGITAL SELECTIVE CALLING 45

Distress alert	47
Undesignated or designated distress alerts	48
Receipt and acknowledgement of DSC alerts	49
Distress alert relay	51
Urgency call	51
Safety call	51
Routine call	53
DSC priorities or call categories	53
Classes of DSC controller	54
Cancelling false alerts	54
Avoiding false alerts	55
Questions	55
Answers	57

6 DSC AND RADIOTELEPHONY PROCEDURES 59

Distress	59
On-scene communications	63
Procedural words relating to distress working	63
Distress relay	64
Urgency	65
Safety	65
Routine procedures	66
Contacting a vessel whose MMSI is unknown	67
Questions	68
Answers	70

7 THE RADIOTELEPHONY EXAMINATION 73

8 THE INMARSAT SYSTEMS 81

INMARSAT C	83
INMARSAT Fleet F77	83
Operations	84
Two-digit special service codes	85
Distress priority connections on Fleet F77	86
Distress alerting on SAT C	86
Avoiding false alerts	86
Cancelling false alerts	86
Security	87
Questions	87
Answers	88

9 INMARSAT PROCEDURES 89

Fleet F77	89
Priority connections	89
Distress priority connection by telephone	89
Distress message by telephone	90
Distress relay connection	90
Urgency priority connection	90

Urgency message by telephone · · · · · · · · · · · 90
Safety priority connection · · · · · · · · · · · · · · 91
Safety message by telephone · · · · · · · · · · · 91
Routine priority connection · · · · · · · · · · · · · 92
INMARSAT C · 92
Distress alerting · 92
Distress message · 93
Other priority messages · · · · · · · · · · · · · · · · · 94
Logging out · 94
Questions · 95
Answers · 96

10 EPIRBs AND SARTs **98**
EPIRBs · 98
Activation · 101
SARTs · 101
AIS-SART · 103
Testing of EPIRBs and SARTs · · · · · · · · · · 104
Avoiding false alerts · · · · · · · · · · · · · · · · · · · 104
Questions · 105
Answers · 106

11 ANTENNAE AND BATTERIES **107**
VHF antenna · 107
MF and HF whip antenna · · · · · · · · · · · · · · 109
Wire aerial · 109
Antennae for INMARSAT Fleet F77 · · · · · · 110
Antennae for INMARSAT C · · · · · · · · · · · · · 110
Maintenance of antennae · · · · · · · · · · · · · · 111
Batteries · 111
Battery maintenance · · · · · · · · · · · · · · · · · · 112
Questions · 113
Answers · 114

12 MARITIME SAFETY INFORMATION **115**
Navtex · 115
Message types · 116
FEC · 119
Enhanced Group Calling (EGC) · · · · · · · · · 119
Questions · 121
Answers · 122

13 QUICK REFERENCE GUIDE **123**

INDEX · 126

Preface

In 1988 The Global Maritime Distress and Safety System (GMDSS) was incorporated into the 1974 Safety Of Life At Sea (SOLAS) regulations. This 1988 amendment came into force on 1 February 1992 and became mandatory from 1 February 1999 for compulsorily fitted craft. These are vessels over 300 GRT and passenger vessels on international voyages.

In the transition the percentage of false distress alerts rose alarmingly. A false distress alert is one that has been inadvertently sent. Many of these could be directly attributed to poorly designed equipment and lack of sufficient training. Radio Officers are no longer being trained. In many cases, the responsibility for communications has been added to that of the Deck Officer.

Equipment design has been addressed by the introduction of more specific guidelines for manufacturers. There is no plan to recall the preceding generations of equipment already installed on board vessels. However, the International Maritime Organization (IMO) has urged the use of dedicated protected distress buttons and modification of existing equipment where necessary. Training courses are intensive, making it possible to instruct students on only one or two designs of equipment. It is, therefore, imperative to stress that users, once qualified, should take the time to read their instruction manuals and learn how to use the specific equipment on board their vessels. Diligence and awareness can prevent false alerts.

Class D VHF and Class E MF/HF Digital Selective Calling (DSC) controllers have been produced for commercial fishermen and non-SOLAS regulated vessels, as well as leisure craft, whose owners wish to benefit from the GMDSS. It is just as important for users of this equipment to gain training and an insight into the system as a whole to ensure that distress alerts are not sent in error.

Examination syllabi for the GMDSS General Operator's Certificate (GOC), Long Range Certificate (LRC) and Restricted Operator's Certificate (ROC) are covered within this book, as simply as possible. Although the text covers more detail than is required for the ROC examination, it is hoped that readers will gain a valuable insight into the system as a whole. Candidates embarking on GOC and LRC training courses will benefit greatly from reading the text in advance. It can then be used as a focused study guide during the course and an aide memoire once qualified.

Glossary of Abbreviations

AIS-SART	Automatic Identification System – Search And Rescue Transmitter
ADRS	Admiralty Digital Radio Signals
ALRS	Admiralty List of Radio Signals
AMVER	Automated Mutual-assistance VEssel Rescue system
AORE	Atlantic Ocean Region East
AORW	Atlantic Ocean Region West
ARQ	Automatic Repeat on reQuest (one to one telex mode)
ATU	Antenna Tuning Unit
CRS	Coast Radio Station
CS	Coast Station
CQ	An abbreviation for All Stations
DE	An abbreviation for This Is
DSC	Digital Selective Calling
EGC	Enhanced Group Calling
EPIRB	Emergency Position Indicating Radio Beacon
EU	Electronic Unit
EUMETSAT	EUropean organisation for the exploitation of METeorological SATellites
FEC	Forward Error Correction (telex mode for distress working and Navtex)
GEO	Geostationary Earth Orbit
GHz	Gigahertz (1000 MHz)
GMDSS	Global Maritime Distress and Safety System
GPS	Global Positioning System
GRT	Gross Registered Tonnage
H24	Continuous service
H3E	Single sideband with full carrier
HF	High Frequency 3–30 MHz
HX	No fixed hours or specific intermittent hours
IMO	International Maritime Organization
IOR	Indian Ocean Region
ISDN	Integrated Services Digital Network (used for F77)
ITU	International Telecommunications Union
J3E	Single sideband with suppressed carrier
kHz	Kilohertz (1000 Hz)
LEO	Low altitude Earth Orbit
LES	Land Earth Station (can be called a Coast Earth Station)
LUT	Local User Terminal
MCA	Maritime and Coastguard Agency
MCC	Mission Control Centre
MEO	Medium altitude Earth Orbit

MES	Mobile Earth Station (can be called a Ship Earth Station)
MF	Medium Frequency 300–3000 kHz
MHz	Megahertz (1000 kHz)
MID	Maritime Identification Digits
MMSI	Maritime Mobile Service Identity
MPDS	Mobile Packet Data Service (used for F77)
MRCC	Maritime Rescue Co-ordination Centre
MSI	Maritime Safety Information
NCS	Network Co-ordination Station
NOAA	National Oceanic and Atmospheric Administration
POR	Pacific Ocean Region
PTT	Press To Talk
PVT	Performance Verification Test (Sat C)
R3E	Single sideband with reduced pilot carrier
RT	RadioTelephony – ie voice communications
Rx	Receiver
SAR	Search And Rescue
SART	Search And Rescue Transponder
SOLAS	Safety Of Life At Sea
SSB	Single SideBand
TDM	Time-Division Multiplexing
Tx	Transmitter
UTC	Universal Time, Co-ordinated
VHF	Very High Frequency 30–300 MHz (Marine VHF 156–174 MHz)

ACKNOWLEDGEMENTS

Special thanks to Jake Kavanagh, Gill Norton, Kevin Walsh, Stan Bréhaut and Marion Bréhaut for their time and encouragement.

Illustrations by Dave Saunders.

Cartoon (page 1) by Jake Kavanagh.

Computer graphics by Stan Bréhaut.

Photographs: Page 33 Luke Duggan; Page 43 Jotron UK Ltd; page 46 (both images) Electrotech Australia, www.electrotech.net.au; Page 49 JSASTC; Page 54 Standard Horizon; Page 56 Icom UK Ltd; Page 65 Electrotech Australia, www.electrotech.net.au; Page 84 JSASTC; Page 91 Electrotech Australia, www. electrotech.net.au; Page 93 Denise Bréhaut; Page 99 Sartech Engineering Ltd; Page 102 Jotron UK Ltd; Page 104 Kannad Marine; Page 108 (top) Jake Kavanagh; Page 108 (bottom) Denise Bréhaut; Page 115 McMurdo.

Thank you to all concerned for providing photo opportunities.

SafetyNET and FleetNET are service marks of INMARSAT.

1 Introduction to the Systems

In 1979 the International Maritime Organisation (IMO) Assembly overviewed the existing maritime distress and safety system. In the light of technological advances, it was decided to create a new Global Maritime Distress and Safety System (GMDSS) to improve the safety of life at sea.

The old system was based on coast stations and certain classes of vessels maintaining a continuous listening watch on nominated distress frequencies. These vessels were also required to carry basic communications equipment with a working range of approximately 150 nautical miles. Vessels in distress offshore were therefore reliant on nearby shipping to provide assistance.

The new system, which came into force in 1992, incorporated satellites and digital selective calling technology, enabling distress alerts to be received automatically over great distances.

Despite some students finding the technology and procedures daunting, it is important to remember that the difference with GMDSS is that there are now more ways of alerting Maritime Rescue Co-ordination Centres (MRCCs) and other authorities to a maritime incident (see Figure 1 on page 12). Many of these options are more reliable than the old methods and because of the use of technologically advanced equipment, specialist knowledge is not required to operate it. You do not need to know how a TV recorder produces a copy of a television programme but it is imperative that you are able to program it to record a specific item or the technology is wasted. In the same way, you only need an understanding of the GMDSS, along with basic knowledge of how to operate the equipment relating to each system without sending false alerts.

Comparatively few years ago, the only means of calling for assistance at sea was by terrestrial VHF or MF radio. Small craft only had the option of VHF radio until the 1979 Fastnet disaster prompted the production of smaller long range communications equipment. In communications prior to 1999, satellites were only used for the Emergency Position Indicating Radio Beacon (EPIRB). Now the INMARSAT satellites enable near global communications whilst at sea. Digital Selective Calling (DSC), the latest introduction to the GMDSS, has provided a reliable means of terrestrial alerting. Today even the smallest craft can choose to participate in the GMDSS and benefit from improved communications and enhanced search and rescue facilities.

One major change has been the equipment requirements for compulsorily fitted vessels. The old regulations were designed around the size of the ship, with 300 GRT and 1600 GRT being the two main categories. In the GMDSS, trading

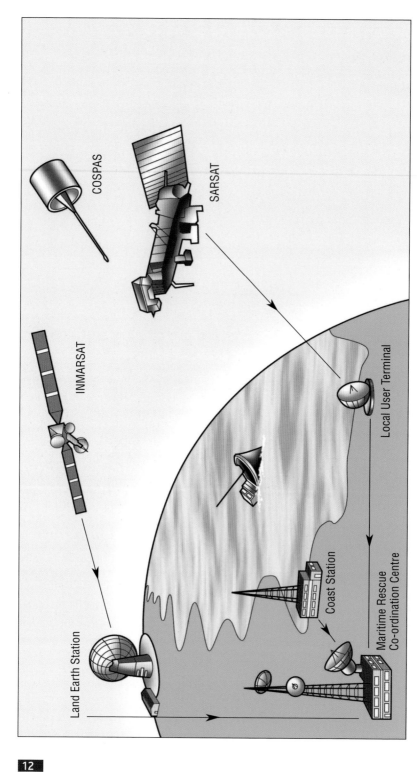

FIG 1 The general concept of GMDSS. There are now several ways of alerting a Maritime Rescue Co-ordination Centre to the fact that a vessel needs assistance. It is then the job of the MRCC to co-ordinate the rescue operations and SAR facilities.

areas determine the equipment requirements, not the size of the vessel. Sea areas one to four are used to define these trading areas (see Figure 2 for sea areas in north-west Europe).

SEA AREAS

A1 is an area within the radiotelephone coverage of at least one VHF coast station operating DSC equipment. Approximately 30–40 mile range.

A2 is an area within the radiotelephone coverage of at least one MF coast station operating DSC equipment, excluding A1 areas. Approximately 150 mile range.

A3 is an area within the coverage of at least one INMARSAT geostationary satellite (between 76° north and south), excluding A1 and A2 areas.

A4 covers the Polar Regions and excludes A1, A2 and A3 areas.

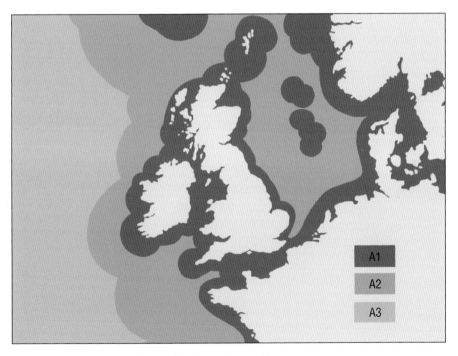

FIG 2 The sea areas A1 and A2 and A3 in north-west Europe.

EQUIPMENT REQUIREMENTS FOR COMPULSORILY FITTED VESSELS

Area A1

Vessels trading exclusively in an A1 area are required to carry a VHF transceiver with channels 16, 13, 06 and those suitable for public correspondence. In addition, they need DSC equipment that is capable of transmitting and watch keeping on channel 70.

Area A2

Vessels trading in A2 areas are required to carry the A1 equipment plus an MF transceiver with 2182 kHz and public correspondence frequencies for telephone or telex. In addition, DSC equipment is required that is capable of transmitting and watch keeping on 2187.5 kHz.

Area A3

Vessels trading in A3 areas are required to carry the A1 and A2 equipment plus one of the following options:

The INMARSAT option

Equipment is required that provides telex alerting, watch keeping and public correspondence by telex or telephone. INMARSAT C meets all of these requirements. Ships are now able to choose to trade deep sea without carrying HF radio equipment.

The HF option

This option requires the installation of an HF transceiver providing radiotelephony and radiotelex. In addition, an HF DSC controller is required with scanning watch keeping on 4207.5, 6312, 8414.5, 12577 and 16804.5 kHz.

Area A4

Vessels trading in A4 areas are required to carry the equipment for areas A1, A2 and the A3 HF option.

All sea areas

In addition to the above, all vessels are required to carry a Navtex receiver for the reception of Maritime Safety Information (MSI). If trading is primarily in an area outside the coverage of Navtex, MSI should be obtained through the INMARSAT SafetyNET service, which is available through INMARSAT C. All vessels should carry a satellite Emergency Position Indicating Radio Beacon (EPIRB) in a float free mounting, transmitting on 406 MHz. Two Search and Rescue Transponders (SARTs) are required, along with three handheld VHF radios if over 500 GRT and two if between 300 and 500 GRT.

VOLUNTARILY FITTED VESSELS

The fitting of GMDSS equipment to leisure craft is optional. However, all craft, regardless of size, are advised to carry a VHF radio. Handheld or transportable VHF radios are sufficient for very small craft staying within five nautical miles of land. They are also useful as an additional piece of safety equipment. Fixed VHF radios are advisable for larger vessels venturing further afield. The transmitter power output is greater and the aerial is higher, enabling communications at a greater range. A VHF DSC controller is a useful piece of equipment to carry and may even become essential if coast stations cease to keep a listening watch on channel 16. An EPIRB, SART, MF radio and MF DSC controller are advisable on board a vessel that may travel up to 150 nautical miles from a safe haven. INMARSAT systems may be considered by larger craft on longer passages as an alternative to HF radio. Navtex is a convenient way to receive weather and navigational information without listening to the various transmissions that are available from other sources.

Questions

1 To which vessels do the GMDSS regulations apply?

2 Define GMDSS sea area A1.

3 Define GMDSS sea area A2.

4 Define GMDSS sea area A3.

5 Define GMDSS sea area A4.

Answers

1 The regulations apply to vessels over 300 GRT and passenger vessels on international voyages.

2 Sea area A1 is an area within the radiotelephone coverage of at least one VHF coast station operating DSC equipment. Approximately 30–40 mile range.

3 Sea area A2 is an area within the radiotelephone coverage of at least one MF coast station operating DSC equipment, excluding A1 areas. Approximately 150 mile range.

4 Sea area A3 is an area within the coverage of at least one INMARSAT geostationary satellite, excluding A1 and A2 areas.

5 Sea area A4 covers the Polar Regions and excludes A1, A2 and A3 areas.

2 UK Training Courses and Examinations

THE GENERAL OPERATOR'S CERTIFICATE COURSE (GOC)

The GMDSS General Operator's Certificate is the most advanced of the courses covered within this text. In the UK most course providers will offer either a straight seven-day course prior to the examination, or seven weekdays with the weekend free for private study. Any course will be intensive, with homework required in the evenings. Candidates will be at an advantage if they do some pre-course learning and keyboard familiarity is essential. A course is compulsory for access to the examination.

THE GOC EXAMINATION

The examination structure is constantly being reviewed and revised. The following information is a guide to the UK examination at the time of writing. It should also be noted that other administrations have different examination structures. The GOC examination consists of three sections:

1. The General Knowledge paper

The paper consists of a written section of three SOLAS questions based on distress, urgency and safety, which must be passed. There are also 12 multiple-choice questions about the radio regulations in general. 12 marks are available for each SOLAS answer and one for each multiple-choice. 25 minutes are available to complete the paper. Examiners strictly adhere to the marking scheme and the pass mark is 75%. This paper is one of the major stumbling blocks in the GOC examination and exam technique is very important.

2. The Radiotelephony examination

During the radiotelephony (RT) examination a simulation of RT distress working is conducted. Each candidate is required to respond to transmissions in the appropriate manner. At the same time, all candidates are required to keep radio logs of all transmissions. The examination lasts approximately 30 minutes for a group of eight candidates. Correct recording of positions in the log book is mandatory and the pass mark is 75%. With sufficient practice during the course this examination should be straightforward.

3. The Operational Performance test

This is a practical examination that will be made as realistic as possible. The candidate will be joining a ship and be given a scenario. During the passage, the candidate will be asked to use the MF, HF and VHF transceivers, MF, HF and

VHF DSCs, Navtex, INMARSAT Fleet F77 and INMARSAT C equipment. Knowledge of batteries, EPIRBs and SARTs, along with keyboard skills and the ability to use publications, are also tested. Each candidate is examined individually for up to 90 minutes. The pass mark is 70% with no 'grey box' ticks permitted on the examiner's report. The examiner will award a 'grey box' tick and fail the candidate if, for instance, the candidate cannot perform safety critical operations.

THE LONG RANGE CERTIFICATE (LRC) COURSE

The Long Range Certificate replaces the old Restricted Certificate of Competence in Radiotelephony, often known as the SSB certificate. The LRC certificate has been tailored to meet the needs of non-SOLAS vessels and commercial craft less than 300 GRT. In addition to the LRC, there is an optional satellite module. The LRC course typically lasts four days.

THE LRC EXAMINATION

The examination has three sections:

1. The General Knowledge paper

This may be written or conducted orally. The paper consists of two SOLAS questions based on distress, urgency and safety, which must be passed. There are also 12 multiple-choice questions about the radio regulations in general. The duration of the paper is left to the examiner's discretion. There are 12 marks available for each SOLAS answer and one for each multiple-choice. Examiners strictly adhere to the marking scheme and the pass mark is 75%.

2. The Radiotelephony examination

This follows exactly the same format as the GOC examination above.

3. The Operational Performance test

This is a practical examination that will be made as realistic as possible. The candidate will be joining a ship and be given a scenario. During the passage, the candidate will be asked to use the MF, HF and VHF transceivers, MF, HF and VHF DSCs and the Navtex. Knowledge of batteries, EPIRBs and SARTs, along with the ability to use publications, are also tested. The examination is carried out on an individual basis and may last up to 45 minutes. The pass mark is 70% with no 'grey box' ticks permitted on the examiner's report. The examiner will award a 'grey box' tick and fail the candidate if, for instance, the candidate cannot perform safety critical operations.

SATELLITE MODULE

The satellite module has two sections that may be taken at the same time as the LRC examination, at no extra charge.

1. The General Knowledge paper

This may be written or conducted orally. The paper consists of one SOLAS question, based on distress, urgency and safety, which must be passed, and 8 multiple-choice questions about the radio regulations in general. The duration of the paper is left to the examiner's discretion. There are 12 marks available for the SOLAS answer and one for each multiple-choice. Examiners strictly adhere to the marking scheme and the pass mark is 75%.

2. The Operational Performance test

This is a 15-minute practical examination on the INMARSAT C equipment. The pass mark is 70% with no 'grey box' ticks permitted.

THE RESTRICTED OPERATOR'S CERTIFICATE (ROC) COURSE

The Restricted Operator's Certificate was introduced in 1998. It provides a GMDSS qualification for commercial operators trading exclusively in A1 areas. Many course providers will offer a three-day course prior to the examination.

THE ROC EXAMINATION

This examination has three sections:

1. The General Knowledge paper

This may be written or conducted orally. The paper consists of two SOLAS questions based on distress, urgency and safety, which must be passed. There are also 12 multiple-choice questions about the radio regulations in general. The duration of the paper is left to the examiner's discretion. There are 12 marks available for each SOLAS answer and one for each multiple-choice. Examiners strictly adhere to the marking scheme and the pass mark is 75%.

2. The Radiotelephony examination

This follows exactly the same format as the GOC examination above.

3. The Operational Performance test

This is a practical examination that will be made as realistic as possible. The candidate will be joining a ship and be given a scenario. During the passage, the candidate will be asked to use the VHF transceiver, VHF DSC and Navtex. Knowledge of batteries, EPIRBs and SARTs, along with the ability to use publications, is also tested. The examination is carried out on an individual basis and may last up to 45 minutes. The pass mark is 70% with no 'grey box' ticks permitted on the examiner's report. The examiner will award a 'grey box' tick and fail the candidate if, for instance, the candidate cannot perform safety critical operations.

STCW

All officers who need to comply with the STCW code must have their ROC or GOC GMDSS certificate endorsed by the MCA. After obtaining the STCW endorsement, it must be revalidated every five years. This is done by providing the relevant forms and proving at least one year of sea service in the last five.

3 Modes of Emission and Propagation

There is no requirement to know radio communications theory in detail, either for the examinations or for practical use of the equipment. What follows is therefore a very simple explanation.

MODES OF EMISSION

When the Press To Talk (PTT) switch on the microphone is operated, a carrier is generated. Figure 3 shows the carrier on a frequency spectrum diagram. The vertical axis indicates power or level.

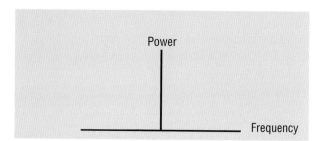

FIG 3 A carrier on a frequency spectrum.

If someone speaks into the microphone when the PTT is held in, voice modulation is superimposed onto each side of the carrier. This produces an upper and lower sideband, which are mirror images of each other and contain identical information. The transmitter power will be shared between the carrier and the sidebands. For example, a fully modulated 400 watt transmitter would radiate a carrier of 267 watts and 66.5 watts in each of the sidebands. The mode represented in Figure 4 is known as A3E, **double sideband with full carrier**.

FIG 4 A3E, double sideband with full carrier.

The human ear can detect audio frequencies from approximately 20 to 25,000 Hz. However, only speech signals between approximately 300 Hz and 3000 Hz (3 kHz) are used in a maritime transmitter. Speech frequencies up to 3 kHz will produce intelligible communications but they will lack personality. As a result, the bandwidth of the modulated carrier is 6 kHz, 3 kHz for each sideband. If we take 2182 kHz as an example, a transmission will use frequencies from 2179 kHz to 2185 kHz, with 2182 kHz being the assigned frequency to which we refer.

We actually only need the upper sideband for maritime communications, so a filter is used from 2179 to 2181.9 kHz to remove the lower sideband. Remember that with the 400 watt transmitter, 267 watts are used to produce the carrier. The remaining 133 watts are now available for use by the upper sideband. The practical result of this is that either the drain on the ship's batteries can be reduced without significant loss of range, or the range of communications can be increased without increasing the power output of the transmitter (see Figure 5).

FIG 5 H3E, single sideband with full carrier.

This mode is known as H3E, **single sideband with full carrier**, sometimes labelled AM, and was always used by ships transmitting on 2182 kHz. This is the only mode that is compatible with A3E. Some survival craft radio equipment used A3E but it became obsolete with the full implementation of GMDSS. H3E is, therefore, no longer used on 2182 kHz.

The ideal situation would be to suppress the carrier completely, making all of the transmitter power available to the upper sideband; 66.5 watts would now produce the same effective radiated power as the original 400 watt transmission using A3E. The carrier must be generated in the transmitter in order to place the audio frequencies in the correct part of the radio frequency spectrum. Once this has been achieved, the carrier is removed by circuitry prior to transmission. The mode represented in Figure 6 is known as J3E, **single sideband with suppressed carrier**, sometimes labelled USB or SSB, now the most frequently used mode in maritime communications.

FIG 6 J3E, single sideband with suppressed carrier.

A receiver cannot detect radio frequency without a full carrier. Much of the expense of a communications receiver is in the circuitry that is necessary to reinsert the carrier. The reinsertion must be in exactly the same place as if the original transmitter had produced it. In some situations, especially with old equipment, a pilot may be needed in order to act as a guide for carrier reinsertion. This pilot is achieved by sending a small amount of carrier. The mode is known as R3E, **single sideband with reduced carrier**. This mode, represented in Figure 7, would only be selected if the receiving station requested it. However, most modern equipment is capable of receiving J3E without any real difficulty.

FIG 7 R3E, single sideband with reduced carrier.

2179   2182   2185 kHz

If the inserted carrier frequency is either too high or too low, the pitch of the received voice signal will be wrong (see Figure 8). The receiving station can modify the frequency of the carrier by use of the **clarifier** or **fine tune** control.

If the carrier is placed here, the low notes will be lost and the voice will sound like Donald Duck.

If the carrier is placed here, the high notes will be lost and the voice will sound like Goofy.

FIG 8 The clarifier or fine tune control in the receiving station is used to modify the frequency in order to clarify speech.

The last modes that you need to know about are those used for radiotelex. F1B is used for radiotelex and DSC on MF and HF. It uses Frequency Shift Keying (FSK), with two carriers separated by just 170 Hz. J2B uses two audio tones to send telex over radio.

To help you remember

A3E All of the carrier and **A**ll of the information.

H3E Was used on 2182 kHz, which was where we called for **H**elp.
Uses the w**H**ole carrier and single sideband.

J3E Just the single sideband, no carrier. Used **J**ust about all the time.

R3E Reduced carrier, single sideband.

PROPAGATION OF THE RADIO WAVE

In free space, electromagnetic waves have both electric and magnetic fields that are always at right angles to each other and the direction of travel. The continual build-up and collapse of these fields is represented in Figure 9 by a sine wave. When the frequency of such electromagnetic waves is suitable for communications by radio, it is referred to as a radio wave. Radio waves travel outwards through the air at a constant speed of approximately 186,000 miles per second, which is the speed of light, in the form of an expanding sphere from an omnidirectional antenna. The wavelength is the distance between two points of repetition, usually measured in metres. The wavelength of 156.8 MHz (VHF channel 16), for example, is 1.91 metres and that of 2182 kHz is 137.5 metres.

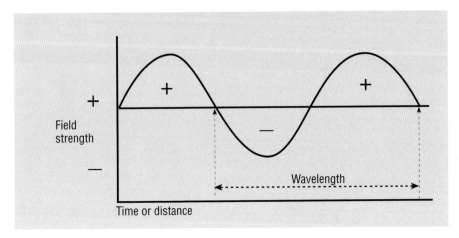

FIG 9 A sine wave.

The frequency is the number of waves that pass a given point in a given amount of time, usually measured in cycles per second or Hertz (Hz). The wavelength of channel 16 (VHF, Very High Frequency) is smaller than that of 2182 kHz (MF, Medium Frequency). If speed is constant, more 1.91 metre units will pass a given point in a given time than 137.5 metre units in the same time, therefore we can deduce that the frequency must be higher.

Some students find the relationship between kHz, MHz and GHz confusing.

To help you remember			
1 kHz =	1,000 Hz		
1 MHz =	1,000 kHz	= 1,000,000 Hz	
1 GHz =	1,000 MHz	= 1,000,000 kHz	= 1,000,000,000 Hz
2182 kHz can also be referred to as being 2.182 MHz, in the 2 MHz band.			

The ionosphere

The existence of ionised layers in the atmosphere was not realised until the 1920s, when radio communications over long distances were achieved using HF (High Frequency) propagation. These layers are now collectively called the ionosphere. As X-rays and ultraviolet radiation from the sun enter the upper atmosphere, they strip electrons from atoms and molecules present in these layers. The electrons are negatively charged and the remaining atoms become positively charged due to the loss of the electrons. These positively charged atoms are known as ions, hence the naming of the ionosphere. Due to the electromagnetic nature of radio waves, this charged layer can affect their propagation. The effect takes the form of refraction, meaning that radio waves entering the ionosphere will have their paths bent. If enough bending occurs, the wave will be refracted back to earth.

The distance covered between the transmitter and the point of possible reception of the returning wave in a single hop is known as the Skip Distance. The geographical area where the transmission cannot be received is called the Dead Zone. The higher the frequency of the radio wave, the more ions are required to refract it and return it to earth. As frequency increases, the amount of bending decreases and frequencies greater than approximately 30 MHz will penetrate the ionosphere relatively unaffected and escape into space (see Figure 10).

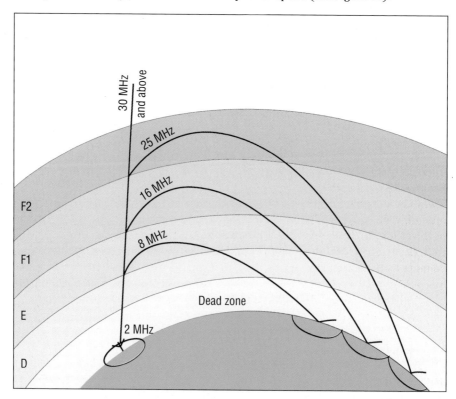

FIG 10 Propagation by day.

Three separate layers are recognisable within the ionosphere. The D layer occurs below 55 miles, the E layer between 55 and 100 miles and the F layer, which is subdivided into F1 and F2, above this altitude. These layers are not constant but fluctuate with, for example, time of day or season and are extremely variable during the 11-year sun spot cycle. When the sun's radiation is strong, HF propagation is better because there are more ions present in the ionosphere. Some stations produce propagation prediction charts that take these anomalies into consideration.

Since ionisation is primarily caused by incoming solar radiation, the number of free electrons and ions increases with altitude and decreases in all layers at night. Refraction at a higher level within the ionosphere will produce greater skip distances and also greater dead zones. The maritime community is allocated parts of the spectrum in the 4, 6, 8, 12, 16, 22 and 26 MHz bands. Each band will be affected differently by the ionosphere.

The F2 layer contains the highest ion density and refracts high HF radio waves. The F1 layer is less ionised and refracts radio waves in the mid HF range. The use of these layers will enable communications over approximately 2500 to 2000 miles respectively with one hop. At night the two layers combine to form a single F layer.

Within the E layer the ion density is lower still and is responsible for refracting lower HF frequencies, enabling communications over approximately 1500 miles with one hop.

The D layer is of special interest. The air itself is denser but contains the lowest level of ionisation. Frequencies below 3 MHz, which include MF radio waves, are weakened or disappear in this layer during the day due to the activity between the molecules of the air and the electrons. The D layer is most active around mid-day. However, at night, when there are fewer ions, these waves can pass through unaffected, to be refracted in the layers above.

TYPES OF RADIO WAVES

Each radio transmission propagates in three distinct modes, one of which will always be dominant depending on the frequency involved. The three modes are a ground wave, a sky wave and a direct wave. Ground waves follow the curvature of the earth and because of their proximity to the ground they lose their energy to it, producing a usable range of approximately 150 to 200 miles. Long-distance communications are achieved by the use of sky waves that are refracted by the ionosphere and returned to earth. Several skips are possible, which will enable communications over many thousands of miles. Direct waves are used for communications over short distances, directly from one aerial to another.

Ground wave

The ground wave range becomes shorter as frequency becomes higher. MF uses primarily the ground wave and the range is mainly dependent on transmitter power output. During the day, approximately one kilometre of range for every watt of radiated power can be expected. However, during the night, as we have

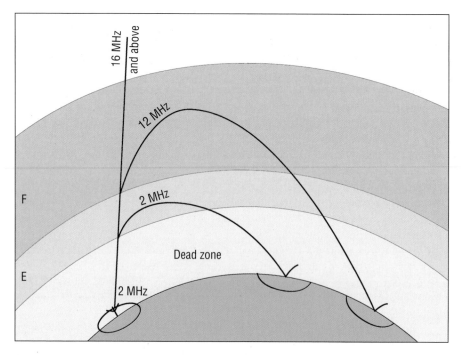

FIG 11 Propagation at night.

seen, the sky wave becomes more usable. 2182 kHz transmissions can therefore increase from around 150 miles during the day using the ground wave to about 1000 miles at night using the sky wave (see Figure 11).

Sky wave

The HF ground wave range is limited to a few miles, so the sky wave is used to enable world-wide communications. Range is dependent on the propagation path rather than transmitter power output. The higher the frequency that can be used, the greater the range as the attenuation (weakening) of the radio wave is less and the skip distance is greater. To work out an appropriate frequency for use, make an estimate, using a propagation prediction chart if available. This will take the path length between the two stations into consideration, along with the daylight/ night-time conditions. When using HF, the daylight frequency will be approximately twice the night-time frequency. For example, from the Indian Ocean to the UK, 22 MHz might be used for an all daylight path and 8 MHz for an all night-time path. If the path is a mixture of daytime and night-time, the frequency will be constrained by the night-time path and 12 MHz might be appropriate. At certain times, long distance east to west communications can be limited to a very short window, maybe only a few hours each day. Listen to your estimated frequency; if there is no working, wait for a traffic list or listen to the telex frequency of the coast station, where a continuous transmission of their callsign in Morse will be heard. If reception is good, this band is suitable for radiotelephony communications; if not, try another. The ability to work out propagation paths will improve with practice and is a skill worth achieving. Instead of calling a European coast radio station on VHF requesting an expensive link call to America, an operator could work out the path, call America direct on HF and only pay for a local link call.

> ## To help you remember
>
> As frequency increases, distance increases.
>
> Frequencies come **D**own in the **D**ark.
>
> Frequencies above 12 MHz are generally not usable at night.

Direct wave

VHF is said to use a direct wave, producing a line of sight transmission. The ground wave produced by a VHF wave is not usable and the sky wave is not refracted by the ionosphere and returned to earth. At full power, the range of VHF communications is determined only by the height of the two aerials involved. For example, up to 60 nautical miles could be achieved between a ship and a coast station, but only in the region of 15 nautical miles between two yachts and much less between two small fishing boats (see Figure 12). Greater ranges can be achieved between ships and search and rescue aircraft because of their altitude.

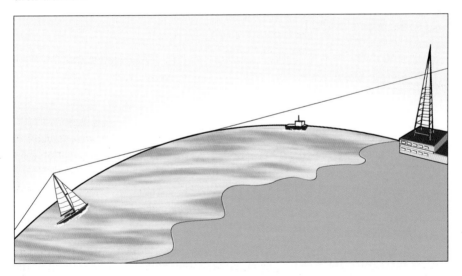

FIG 12 VHF propagation is by direct wave that enables communications within line of sight. In this example the yacht could not communicate with the small fishing vessel.

Space wave

Ultra High Frequency (UHF) uses a direct wave. When used for INMARSAT communications, 1.5/1.6 GHz, it is sometimes referred to as a space wave. This wave is hardly affected by the ionosphere; however, heavy snow or rainfall can adversely affect it.

PRACTICAL USES WITHIN RADIO FREQUENCY BANDS

Low Frequency LF 30 to 300 kHz	198 kHz Radio 4 – 'long wave'
Medium Frequency MF 300 kHz to 3 MHz	Medium range maritime communications. Navtex.
High Frequency HF 3 to 30 MHz	World-wide maritime communications.
Very High Frequency VHF 30 to 300 MHz	Short range maritime communications. (Marine VHF is 156–174 MHz.)
Ultra High Frequency UHF 300 MHz to 3 GHz	EPIRBs and INMARSAT communications. GPS position fixing system.
Super High Frequency SHF 3 to 30 GHz	Radar and SARTs.

As the frequency increases, the wavelength decreases. Low frequency wavelengths can be in excess of one kilometre, whereas the super high frequency wavelength is only a few centimetres.

To help you remember

Picture the radio wave entering the ionosphere and colliding with the free electrons and ions. The smaller the wavelength, the smaller the chance of collision. VHF and UHF radio waves can, therefore, escape the ionosphere and be used for satellite communications.

Questions

1 What do you understand by the mode A3E?

2 What do you understand by the mode H3E?

3 When was H3E used?

4 What do you understand by the mode J3E?

5 What do you understand by the mode R3E?

6 When would R3E be used?

7 What function does the clarifier or fine tune control have?

8 What is a dead zone?

9 Which layers exist in the ionosphere during the day?

10 Which layers can be used in the ionosphere during the night?

11 Which mode of propagation do you associate with MF transmissions?

12 Which mode of propagation do you associate with HF transmissions?

13 Which mode of propagation do you associate with VHF transmissions?

14 Which mode of propagation do you associate with UHF transmissions?

Answers

1 A3E has a full carrier and double sideband.

2 H3E has a full carrier and single sideband.

3 H3E was used on 2182 kHz.

4 J3E has a single sideband with suppressed carrier.

5 R3E has a single sideband with reduced carrier.

6 R3E would only be used if the receiving station requested it.

7 The clarifier or fine tune is used to clarify the received voice by slightly altering the frequency of the carrier reinsertion.

8 A dead zone is the geographical area between the transmitter and returning sky wave where the transmission cannot be received by any station.

9 During the day D, E, F1 and F2 layers exist in the ionosphere.

10 During the night the D layer becomes very weak; however, the E layer and the combined F layers can be used.

11 MF is associated with ground wave propagation. However, at night, sky wave propagation may also be used.

12 HF is associated with sky wave propagation.

13 VHF uses direct wave propagation.

14 UHF uses direct wave propagation that is often called a space wave.

4 General Regulations and Procedures

The Radio Regulations are agreed at meetings of the World Administrative Radio Council (WARC), which is part of the International Telecommunications Union (ITU), which is itself part of the United Nations (UN). Each country has an administrative body in place to police the regulations by controlling the licensing and operation of ship radio installations. In the United Kingdom, the Maritime and Coastguard Agency (MCA), part of the Department of Transport, is responsible for marine radio matters. The Association of Marine Electronic and Radio Colleges (AMERC) carries out examinations and certification of operators for the ROC, LRC and GOC on behalf of the MCA. The Office of Communications (Ofcom) issues Ship Radio Licences and Maritime Mobile Service Identity (MMSI) numbers. Appropriate authorities can inspect operators' certificates and the radio installation at any time, either at home or abroad. Poor radio equipment found during such inspections may be confiscated. Breach of the radio regulations may result in the authority to operate being suspended or revoked.

The Master, or person responsible for the vessel, has absolute authority over the radio installation. Operators use the radio equipment under the authority of the Master. However, the operators are still responsible for the correct use of the equipment. Unlicensed persons may use the radio installation under the supervision of a licensed operator. It should be noted that Section 11 of the 1884 Post Office Protection Act applies. This Act forbids the reception of communications, other than those for which the station is licensed. If such communications are unwittingly received, they must not be revealed in any way.

IDENTIFICATION OF STATIONS

Every transmission must include the station's identification. Ships at sea and coast stations on land are usually referred to by name. Coast Radio Stations (CRS) are named after the geographical location of the antenna followed by the word 'radio'. For example, Malaga Radio has its antenna situated at Malaga. Coastguard stations are named after the area that they control. For example, Solent Coastguard controls the Solent area.

In addition, if a station operates licensed communications equipment, it will be allocated an international callsign, which is an alphanumeric identifier that is unique to it, similar to the registration number of a car. The first letter identifies the country of registration. The UK allocations are G, M or 2, therefore MLXE8 would belong to a UK vessel. If a vessel changes hands but stays with the same flag, it will keep its callsign, in the same way that a car would keep its registration number.

Survival craft stations may use the callsign of the parent ship, followed by an extra two digits, which should not be 0 or 1 if immediately following a letter.

The GMDSS has introduced a new type of identification known as the Maritime Mobile Service Identity (MMSI), which is a **nine-digit** identity with no letters. The Maritime Identification Digits (MID) are three digits within the MMSI that identify the country of registration. The UK allocation is 232, 233, 234 and 235. A ship's MMSI is made up of the three-digit MID followed by its own six-digit identity. The coast station MMSI is made up of 00, then the MID, followed by the coast station's four-digit identity. An MMSI used by a group of ships is made up of 0, then the MID, followed by the five-digit group identity. If a ship has a group MMSI, it will also have an individual MMSI. SAR aircraft have a nine digit MMSI commencing triple one.

Example of MMSI numbers

Ship **MMSI**	123 123456
Coast station MMSI	**00** 123 1234
Group MMSI	**0** 123 12345
SAR aircraft	**111** 123 123

Finally, we have the INMARSAT mobile identification numbers. Students should remember the total number of digits and the leading digit for each system.

Example of INMARSAT mobile numbers

INMARSAT C	**nine** digits commencing **four**	423264763
INMARSAT Fleet F77	**nine** digits commencing **seven**	764092849

RADIO WATCH

Since 1st February 1999 there has been no requirement to keep a listening watch on 2182 kHz. All ships now maintain a continuous watch by DSC instead. However, ships will continue to maintain a listening watch on VHF channel 16.

Ships may have many different communication systems, each having its own identification.

DSC WATCH KEEPING

- Ships in sea area A1 should monitor channel 70.
- Ships in sea area A2 should monitor channel 70, plus 2187.5 kHz.
- Ships in sea areas A3 and A4 should monitor channel 70, 2187.5 kHz, 8414.5 kHz plus at least one other HF distress, urgency and safety frequency.

Ships in sea area A3 that have taken the INMARSAT option are not required to monitor the HF DSC frequencies. Owners of leisure craft who do not wish to join in the GMDSS should continue to keep watch on channel 16 and 2182 kHz for the time being. Some countries, including the UK, have stated that they intend to keep a listening watch for the foreseeable future. Other countries have decided to discontinue the listening watch on 2182 kHz. There is little doubt that all shore stations will discontinue it at some point in the future, at which time leisure craft owners may feel it to be prudent to install GMDSS equipment on board.

TEST TRANSMISSIONS

The operators responsible for testing the radio equipment are listed in Section B of the ship's GMDSS log book. Tests of radio transmitters must last less than 10 seconds, must include the identity of the station, should avoid channel 16 and 2182 kHz, and use low power or an artificial antenna (dummy load) if possible. A test call is a system test that does not require a response from any other station. If there is doubt regarding the ability of the transceiver to function correctly, another station should be involved. Do this by requesting a radio check, which is asking for advice about the strength and quality of the signal. The following tests are important during examinations and in practice:

Every day, the system self test should be carried out on the DSC controller. This does not require signals to be radiated, it just checks the internal circuitry of the unit. Battery voltage should be tested and the battery charged if required. Printers should be checked to ensure an adequate supply of paper.

Each week, the external test should be carried out on the DSC controller. This is a special test call to a coast station on MF or HF, taking the safety priority. There is not usually any operator involvement, as a computer system will recognise the test call format and automatically send back a DSC acknowledgement. There is not always an automatic test call facility for VHF DSC. This equipment should be tested, if necessary, by sending a routine DSC call to another station. Reserve sources of energy should be checked.

Every month, the EPIRB and SARTs should be tested, along with a more thorough check on the ship's antennae and batteries (see Chapters 10 and 11 for more details). Survival craft VHF radios should be tested on board using a working channel and the reserve primary battery should be in date with an unbroken seal.

When the tests have been carried out, an entry should be made in the GMDSS log book and the operator who carried out the tests should sign against it. When making such entries, always use UTC for time keeping.

DOCUMENTS

Students should be aware of the documents that are listed opposite. Pay particular attention to the ALRS/ADRS, as candidates will be expected to extract information from these during the practical examination. One mistake many students make is in not remembering that if, for example, the coast station receives on 2009 kHz, calling stations must transmit on that frequency in order for the coast station to be able to receive them. Any entry in bold type is the preferred channel or frequency. Quite often there are very small figures next to an entry (remember to take your spectacles), which refer to notes that should always be read before choosing a channel or frequency. The hours of watch keeping are also listed. H24 means a 24-hour watch.

Admiralty List of Radio Signals (ALRS) and Admiralty Digital Radio Signals (ADRS)

Volume 1 comes in 2 parts and lists the working arrangements of maritime radio stations.

Volume 2 provides information regarding radio navigational aids, including time signals.

Volume 3 comes in 2 parts and contains details of radio weather services and navigational warnings.

Volume 4 lists meteorological observation stations.

Volume 5 is the GMDSS volume and will be of interest to all students.

Volume 6 comes in 8 parts and provides information regarding port operations, pilot services, Vessel Traffic Services (VTS) and reporting systems.

International Telecommunications Union (ITU) Publications

Details of ships can be obtained from the ITU **List of Ship Stations and Maritime Mobile Service Identity Assignments.** Coast Station information is found in the **List of Coast Stations and Special Service Stations**. Both are available in CD-ROM format.

International Code of Signals

The International Code of Signals could be used when communicating with an operator who speaks a different language. For example, during communications regarding a medical emergency, 'Mike Golf India' would indicate that 'the patient is suffering from non-corrosive poisoning (no staining and burning of mouth and lips)'.

TRANSMISSIONS IN UK HARBOURS

Each country has its own regulations for the use of radio equipment in its waters. Details can be found in ALRS/ADRS Volume 1. UK regulations permit communications with the nearest coast station, which restricts communications to the use of VHF. Broadcast messages may be received and any port operations or private channels for which the vessel is licensed may be used.

SIMPLEX AND DUPLEX

Simplex is a method of communicating in which either reception or transmission is possible at any one time. A PTT (Press To Talk) switch is used to transmit and when it is released the receiver will operate. Duplex working allows transmission and reception simultaneously, as with the telephone system, but in the case of MF/HF, it must have two separate antennae or, in the case of VHF, it must have a duplex filter system.

A simplex channel is one that uses a single frequency for alternate reception and transmission. When listening to a simplex channel with a VHF radio, you will hear both sides of any communications, providing that both stations are in range.

A duplex channel is one that uses two frequencies, one to transmit and another to receive. Duplex channels are used to communicate from ship to shore. For example, when channel 80 is used, the ship will transmit on 157.025 MHz and in order to hear the transmission, the shore station must receive on that frequency. The shore station transmits its reply on 161.625 MHz and the ship must receive on that frequency. The shore station transceiver is, therefore, programmed with the opposite transmit and receive frequencies to the ship transceiver. When listening to a duplex channel with a VHF radio, only the shore transmissions will be heard and the receiver will be silent during transmissions from other ships. Using the duplex system without being able to transmit and receive simultaneously, as with a marine VHF radio, is termed semi-duplex.

THE USE OF CHANNELS AND FREQUENCIES IN THE MARITIME BAND

There are special channels and frequencies set aside for distress, urgency and safety. All others are termed working channels and frequencies. We will look primarily at the uses of the VHF channels because this is probably the area that is most familiar to readers.

Channel 16   is for radiotelephony communications relating to distress and urgency. Mariners have to monitor channel 16 and it is, therefore, also used as a routine calling channel. This situation will remain for the foreseeable future.

Channel 70   is for distress, urgency, safety and routine announcements by DSC. **Under no circumstances should this channel be used for radiotelephony communications.**

Channel 67   is for small craft safety, the UK Coastguard's working channel. Although named 'small craft safety', the UK Coastguard also deals with the safety of large ships.

Channel 13   is for bridge to bridge safety of navigation by radiotelephony.

The remainder of the 55 channels are allocated for Intership, Public Correspondence and Port Operation uses.

Intership channels

Intership channels must be simplex to enable ships to communicate with each other. Channel 06 is the primary intership channel and 08 the secondary preference. Channels 72 and 77 are used solely for ship to ship communications, making them safe channels to use with no risk of interference to coast stations. If you know that the station with which you wish to communicate is close, try low power first. If you get no response, wait the required time of two minutes and try again on high power.

There will be dedicated intership frequencies in the MF and HF bands. These frequencies will be issued with the ship radio licence. An example of an MF frequency would be 2048 kHz.

Public correspondence channels

Public correspondence channels must be duplex in order to link mariners at sea into the telephone network on land. Most coast radio stations should be called on VHF using full power on their working channels, some of which are computer controlled. However, stations calling on MF can often call on 2182 kHz. Details of working arrangements of coast radio stations can be found in ALRS/ADRS Volume 1, which should always be consulted prior to calling.

Port operation channels

Port operation channels can be either simplex or duplex. Port operations concerning large craft are usually conducted on simplex channels. UK marinas often operate on channel 80, which is a duplex channel. Remember that when other vessels are transmitting on a duplex channel, receivers on board listening vessels will be silent and only the response from the marina will be heard. Because marinas often work the same channel, small craft should call them on low power when they are at close range. If high power is selected, several marinas could hear the call. Southampton VTS operates on channel 12. It is a simplex channel, which is important since all ships should hear transmissions from both ship and shore. Port operation stations deal with the safety of vessels and persons in and out of port and should be called direct on their working channels, details of which can be found in ALRS/ADRS Volume 6.

Channels 15 and 17

Channels 15 and 17 may be used on low power for on board communications. It is important to use correct procedure for all transmissions: the vessel's name and 'control' for the bridge and the vessel's name and one of the phonetics for each of the substations. For example:

```
SARPEDON CONTROL
THIS IS
SARPEDON ALPHA
OVER
```

It is important that this procedure is not abbreviated. It was once common practice to transmit, for example, 'Fo'c'sle this is bridge, drop anchors'. Since the vessel is not identified, a potentially dangerous situation could occur if the wrong vessel's anchors were released.

The many international changes to channels and frequencies brought about by the 2015 World Radio-communication Conference will not affect GMDSS at this time.

TRANSCEIVER FUNCTIONS

A transceiver is a piece of equipment that is capable of both transmitting and receiving. A VHF radio will be in receiving mode unless it is transmitting. To activate the transmitter and disable the receiver, the PTT switch on the microphone must be held in.

Volume

The volume control on a VHF transceiver is sometimes called the **Audio Frequency (AF) gain control** on an MF/HF transceiver. They control the level of sound that comes from the speaker but they have no effect on transmissions.

Power output

The transmitter power output will be either 1 or 25 watts on a VHF transceiver. Greater power will give a better signal level at range. Capture effect means that the strongest signal will be received by a VHF transceiver, to the exclusion of all other signals. Always use the minimum power necessary to effect communication unless in distress, when high power should always be selected.

Squelch

A VHF marine transceiver generates a high level of noise in its receiver circuits. The squelch control is a function of the receiver that suppresses this noise. Adjusting the squelch control as far as possible into the noise will make the receiver as sensitive as possible. There is a school of thought that says this should be done when a distress call is sent so that it is possible to receive responses from the edge of the station's range. However, for routine work an operator would not choose to listen to the noise continually. The control should, therefore, be adjusted back until the noise just stops, for optimum reception. Adjusting the control well past the noise threshold will result in the loss of weak signals. Some radios will have an automatic squelch control.

Dual watch

Dual watch enables the unit to monitor two channels at the same time – usually, channel 16, which takes priority, plus one other of the operator's choice. Again, this is a function of the receiver and the dual watch should always be deselected before transmission. If the dual watch is left on and the PTT switch is depressed, some radios will transmit on channel 16 and some will transmit on the chosen channel.

Channel 16

The channel 16 button, which is often red or blue, may be used in distress situations. This will turn the dual watch or scan function off and should, ideally, give high power for distress working. However, beware, if the low power is selected and the channel 16 button activated, many older radios will stay in low power.

Scan and dimmer controls

The scan control will scan all available channels. The dimmer control is used to reduce the brightness of the display, or turn the light on and off.

MF/HF transceivers

The remaining functions are associated with the MF/HF transceiver.

The **Radio Frequency (RF) gain control**, sometimes called the **sensitivity control**, is used to adjust the amplification (strength) of incoming Radio Frequency signals.

The **Automatic Gain Control (AGC)** automatically increases weak RF signals and reduces strong RF signals, compensates for fading and produces a steady AF output from the speaker.

The **clarifier** or **fine tune** is used to clarify the reception of speech that is distorted. This can be due to a transmission being slightly off frequency, or by inaccurate carrier reinsertion by the receiver. See page 22.

The **mode control** allows the mode of emission or type of modulation to be selected.

MAXIMUM PERMITTED TRANSMITTER POWER

Always use the minimum power necessary for routine communications, in order to give priority to vessels in distress. In times of distress, all stations involved should always select high power. The maximum permitted transmitter powers on ships using marine radio frequencies are:

25 watts for VHF

400 watts for MF

1500 watts (1.5 kilowatts) for HF

THE PHONETIC ALPHABET

Candidates will need to know the phonetic alphabet for all of the examinations. International callsigns are always spoken using the phonetic alphabet. When spelling words, always speak the procedural words 'I spell' before commencing.

Alpha	Bravo	Charlie	Delta	Echo	Foxtrot
Golf	Hotel	India	Juliet	Kilo	Lima
Mike	November	Oscar	Papa	Quebec	Romeo
Sierra	Tango	Uniform	Victor	Whiskey	X-Ray
Yankee	Zulu				

CONTROL OF COMMUNICATIONS

When routine communications are in progress between ship and shore, the shore station is in control, regardless of who made the initial call. In the case of routine ship to ship communications, it is the called ship that controls.

To help you remember
If you are in the bath and the phone rings, it is up to you whether you answer it or stay where you are! You are in control, and the same is true at sea.

MAKING A ROUTINE CALL

The first thing to do is listen, to ensure that your transmissions will not interfere with communications that are already in progress. If calling on Channel 16 or on 2182 kHz, the call should last less than one minute and no routine messages should be passed. The call is made observing the following regulations:

NAME OF THE CALLED STATION not more than three times
    THIS IS
NAME OF THE CALLING STATION not more than three times
    Ending with the word 'OVER'

Once contact has been made, the identifications are only transmitted once. The end of working between stations is indicated by the word 'Out'.

Example of a ship to ship call on a busy channel 16

ARGENT ARGENT ARGENT
THIS IS
SARPEDON SARPEDON SARPEDON
CHANNEL 77
OVER

Reply: SARPEDON THIS IS ARGENT
CHANNEL 77
(Argent is in control and can agree or select another channel)
OUT

On VHF, when conditions are good, the call may be amended to:

NAME OF THE CALLED STATION once
    THIS IS
NAME OF THE CALLING STATION twice
    OVER

Example of a port operations call on a VHF working channel

> SOUTHAMPTON VTS
> THIS IS
> ORIANA ORIANA
> OVER

If there is no response to an initial routine call, the operator should wait two minutes and try again. If there is no response to the second call, wait another two minutes. Further attempts should be made at not less than three-minute intervals.

DIFFICULTY WITH COMMUNICATIONS

If you receive a call and are not certain the call is intended for you, do nothing until the call has been repeated and understood. However, if you receive a call that is definitely intended for you, but you are uncertain of the identity of the calling station, you can reply immediately in the following manner:

> STATION CALLING HOPPY
> THIS IS HOPPY
> GO AHEAD
> OVER

Questions

1 Under whose authority is the on board communications equipment used?

2 Who is responsible for the correct use of the radio installation?

3 How would you recognise:
   a) A coast station's MMSI number?
   b) A group MMSI number?
   c) An SAR aircraft MMSI number?

4 How would you recognise:
   a) An INMARSAT Fleet F77 mobile number?
   b) An INMARSAT C mobile number?

5 What is the maximum duration of a test call?

6 What are the daily tests associated with the radio equipment?

7 What are the weekly tests associated with the radio equipment?

8 What are the monthly tests associated with the radio equipment?

Questions

9 What information is contained within the ALRS/ADRS Volume 1?

10 What information is contained within the ALRS/ADRS Volume 6?

11 What is the difference between simplex and duplex working?

12 May you use VHF channel 70 for radiotelephony transmissions?

13 What is the function of the squelch control?

14 What is a more common name for the AF gain control?

15 What is the function of the RF gain control?

16 What is the function of the AGC?

17 What is the maximum permitted power output of:
a) A VHF transmitter?
b) An MF transmitter?
c) An HF transmitter?

18 Which station controls during routine ship to ship communications?

19 State the procedure for routine calling on VHF when conditions are good.

20 What is the procedure that you should follow if you hear a call but are uncertain the call is for you?

21 What is the procedure that you should follow if you hear a call that is intended for you, but are unsure of the identification of the calling station?

Answers

1 The communications equipment is used under the authority of the Master.

2 The licensed operator is responsible for the correct use of the radio installation.

3 a) A coast station's MMSI would be nine digits commencing 00.
   b) A group MMSI would be nine digits commencing 0.
   c) An SAR aircraft MMSI would be nine digits commencing 111.

4 a) An INMARSAT Fleet F77 mobile number would be nine digits commencing with a seven.
   b) An INMARSAT C mobile number would be nine digits commencing with a four.

5 The maximum duration of a test call is 10 seconds.

6 Every day the internal system self test should be carried out on the DSC controller. Battery voltage should be tested and the battery charged if required. Printers should be checked to ensure an adequate supply of paper.

7 Every week the MF/HF external test should be carried out on the DSC controller. If there is no automatic test call facility for VHF DSC a routine DSC call may be used. Reserve sources of energy should be checked.

8 Every month the EPIRB and SARTs should be tested, along with a more thorough check on the ship's batteries and antennae. Survival craft VHF radios should be tested on board, using a working channel, and the reserve primary battery should be in date with an unbroken seal.

Survival craft VHF radio with reserve battery in sealed packet.

Answers

9 ALRS/ADRS Volume 1 contains details of the working arrangements of maritime radio stations.

10 ALRS/ADRS Volume 6 contains information regarding port operations.

11 Simplex working uses a single frequency and requires the PTT to be pressed in order to transmit and released in order to receive. Duplex working uses two frequencies, one to transmit and the other to receive. Full duplex working permits simultaneous transmission and reception.

12 It is very important not to use channel 70 for radiotelephony because it is the DSC channel.

13 The squelch control is used to reduce background noise to an acceptable level.

14 The AF gain control alters the strength of the audio frequency and is more commonly referred to as the volume control.

15 The RF gain control alters the amplification (strength) of the incoming radio frequency signals.

16 The automatic gain control automatically increases weak RF signals and reduces strong RF signals, compensates for fading and produces a steady AF output from the speaker.

17 The maximum transmitter power output is
a) 25 watts for VHF
b) 400 watts for MF
c) 1500 watts for HF.

18 In ship to ship communications, the called vessel controls.

19 On VHF when conditions are good the call should be:
Name of called station once, this is, name of calling station twice, over.

20 If you hear a call but are uncertain that the call is for you, you should do nothing until the call has been repeated and understood.

21 If you hear a call which is intended for you but are unsure of the identification of the calling station, you should reply immediately:
Station calling ship name, this is ship name, go ahead, over.

4 Digital Selective Calling

In the early 1980s, the original concept of the GMDSS was built around satellite communications and did not include Digital Selective Calling (DSC). However, DSC now plays a large part and has helped to make the GMDSS as a whole far superior to expectations.

The DSC announcement replicates the 'call' in the old voice procedures. It is simply a way of attracting attention without the need for a physical listening watch to be kept. It is a similar concept to a paging device. The digital signal is very stable and range is slightly increased. This is because it is less affected by certain types of noise, the bandwidth is narrow and there is no squelch control within the VHF DSC receiver. Once a station has been contacted using DSC, radiotelephony communications follow in exactly the same way as they would have done in the past.

The DSC controller is programmed with the ship's MMSI and needs an input of the ship's position, which is often provided by an integral GPS. If there is none and the ship has a position fixing system installed, it must be interfaced with the DSC, to keep it constantly updated. If the GPS fails, the position may be entered manually, in which case it should be updated at least every four hours, along with the time that the position was valid. The DSC unit now knows who it is and where it is, enabling a distress alert to be sent very quickly if necessary.

The VHF DSC controller is a separate installation from the MF/HF DSC controller. These controllers do exactly as their name suggests, they control the transceivers. The VHF DSC controller has an independent dedicated receiver that will monitor channel 70 continuously but will only be able to transmit through the VHF transceiver (see Figure 13). Units are usually manufactured as a combined

FIG 13 VHF DSC, now manufactured as a combined unit.

VHF DSC combined unit.

MF/HF DSC combined unit.

DSC/transceiver, but it should not be forgotten that there are still two distinct functions to the equipment.

The MF/HF DSC controller has a scanning receiver that can monitor more than one distress frequency. There is a dedicated DSC distress, urgency and safety frequency in each of the 2, 4, 6, 8, 12 and 16 MHz bands. Some models of equipment will scan all six frequencies, others will monitor 2187.5 kHz and 8414.5 kHz plus at least one other HF frequency. It may be possible to monitor one or more additional frequencies, depending on the equipment design – an example could be the MF DSC routine calling frequency 2177 kHz. The DSC controller will only be able to transmit through the MF/HF transceiver (see Figure 14), which are now combined.

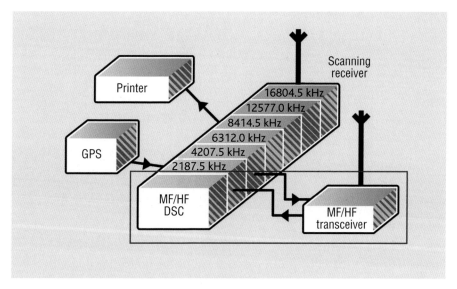

FIG 14 MF/HF DSC, now manufactured as a combined unit.

DISTRESS ALERT

A distress alert will include a minimum of the ship's MMSI number, the position and the time it was valid. Information regarding subsequent communications will also be included. This will be the appropriate radiotelephony or telex frequency that will be in the same band as the original alert. For example, a DSC distress alert received on 2187.5 kHz will either nominate 2182 kHz for radiotelephony communications or 2174.5 kHz for telex working. Most DSC controllers will automatically tune the transceiver to the nominated working channel or frequency once the alert has been received.

These frequencies should be displayed on the bulkhead near the radio installation for practical purposes. However, for the LRC and GOC examinations it is imperative to remember at least those listed in bold.

Distress, urgency and safety frequencies used for DSC, radiotelephony and radiotelex. All MF and HF frequencies are in kHz							
	VHF	MF	HF	HF	HF	HF	HF
DSC	Ch **70**	**2187.5**	4207.5	6312	**8414.5**	12577	16804.5
RT	Ch **16**	**2182**	4125	6215	**8291**	12290	16420
Telex		**2174.5**	4177.5	6268	8376.5	12520	16695

Two ways of alerting exist – a single-frequency attempt and a multi-frequency attempt. The single-frequency attempt will send an alert on the chosen channel or frequency and wait approximately four minutes for a DSC acknowledgement from a coast station. If no acknowledgement is received, another alert is sent and so on, up to a maximum of five times. If the multi-frequency attempt is selected, alerts will be sent automatically on the MF and each of the HF distress frequencies in turn, re-tuning the aerial each time, without waiting for an acknowledgement. Some DSC controllers will send the alert on 2 MHz first, because this will alert the closest stations, followed by 8 MHz, which is the best all-round first choice for HF. Alerts will then be sent on 4, 6, 12 and 16 MHz in turn. Other DSC controllers will send the alerts in sequential order. Again, it is dependent on the equipment design. In either case, if no acknowledgements are received within four minutes, the cycle will begin again.

The multi-frequency attempt is not the best option to take in most circumstances because one or more stations could receive the alert on each of the frequencies. Each station would then listen to the appropriate radiotelephony or telex frequency in the same band in which they received the alert. The vessel in distress would only work on one frequency, either that on which there is a coast station or the one with the nearest ships. Every other station listening on a different HF frequency would, therefore, hear nothing. After five minutes they would be required to relay the information to a coast station and, before long, half the world would be involved. However, if there are only a few minutes available before communications are lost, this is by far the best option to take.

UNDESIGNATED OR DESIGNATED DISTRESS ALERTS

An undesignated distress alert is the quickest type of alert that can be sent. It transmits the minimum amount of information, identity and position, in a matter of seconds. If more time is available, a designated distress alert can be sent giving the nature of the distress selected from a pre-programmed list of designators. These will include:

- FIRE OR EXPLOSION
- FLOODING
- COLLISION
- GROUNDING
- LISTING
- SINKING
- DISABLED AND ADRIFT
- ABANDONING SHIP
- PIRACY OR ATTACK
- MAN OVERBOARD

A GMDSS installation for an offshore leisure craft.

Distress push-buttons are fitted to help combat the high number of false alerts that have been generated within the GMDSS. They have spring-loaded covers that require one hand to lift them and a second hand to press and hold the distress button for either three or five seconds, depending on the manufacturer. Two button systems also exist. All distress buttons should have protective covers.

RECEIPT AND ACKNOWLEDGEMENT OF DSC ALERTS

Once a DSC distress alert has been sent by a vessel, the unit may sound an alarm to warn the crew that a distress alert has been sent but not acknowledged. In an ideal world, the next thing to happen would be the receipt of a DSC acknowledgement from a coast station. The DSC acknowledgement does two things. First, it causes the DSC controller to sound an alarm, telling the vessel in distress that someone is listening on the appropriate radiotelephony frequency for the distress call and message. Second, it prevents the DSC controller from repeating the alert.

When a ship station receives a DSC transmission an alarm will also sound on this unit. The alarm is different for a distress alert and urgency call than it is for a routine call, enabling crew members to tell the difference without having to read the displayed information. Accepting the alert silences this alarm and clears the information to the log, from where it can be retrieved at a later time.

MF or VHF procedure

If a vessel receives a distress alert on MF or VHF, the procedure is to:

- COMMENCE LOG KEEPING AND INFORM THE MASTER
- SET WATCH ON THE APPROPRIATE RADIOTELEPHONY OR TELEX FREQUENCY IN THE SAME BAND
- WAIT A SHORT WHILE FOR A COAST STATION TO ACKNOWLEDGE, IF ONE IS IN RANGE
- ACKNOWLEDGE BY RADIOTELEPHONY
- IF NO RESPONSE OR NO WORKING HEARD, THE ALERT REPEATS AND FIVE MINUTES HAVE PASSED, ACKNOWLEDGE BY DSC
- RELAY THE INFORMATION ASHORE BY ANY MEANS

It is not the responsibility of a vessel to acknowledge by DSC because this would prevent the DSC controller on the vessel in distress from sending more alerts. The requirement is to involve a coast station in the rescue whenever possible. This is why the first response of a ship should be to acknowledge by radiotelephony. If you were in an area covered by a coast station, you would delay this action for a short time to allow the coast station to answer first, exactly as you did in the past with radiotelephony communications. If you were in area A3 and received the alert on channel 70, you would acknowledge immediately. If you were in area A3 and received the alert on 2187.5 kHz, you would acknowledge immediately if the vessel was close, but if not, delay a short time to allow closer vessels to acknowledge first. If the vessel in distress does not respond to your radiotelephony acknowledgement and the alert repeats, you know that there is no shore involvement and there is little option other than to acknowledge by DSC as a last resort.

If you take this action, you must also take it upon yourself to relay the information ashore by whatever means you have available. To avoid congestion of channel 70 in an A1 area, it is not advisable to acknowledge by DSC, unless the alert keeps repeating. The Class D controller does not have the facility to acknowledge by DSC because it is designed for use in A1 areas with good coast station coverage.

HF procedure

If a vessel receives a distress alert on HF, the procedure is:

- COMMENCE LOG KEEPING AND INFORM THE MASTER
- **DO NOT ACKNOWLEDGE**
- SET WATCH ON APPROPRIATE RADIOTELEPHONY OR TELEX FREQUENCY IN THE SAME BAND
- IF NOTHING IS HEARD IN FIVE MINUTES, RELAY ASHORE

The vessel in distress could be halfway round the world and you cannot offer any physical assistance. Therefore, you must not acknowledge receipt of an HF DSC alert.

The flow chart in Figure 15 (on page 52) describes the actions a station should take on receiving a DSC distress alert.

DISTRESS ALERT RELAY

Upon receiving a DSC distress alert relay from another ship, follow the same procedure as for the acknowledgement of a distress alert. However, if the relay is from a coast station on HF and addressed to all ships within a geographic area, the ship should acknowledge by radiotelephony on the appropriate frequency in the same band. This is because it is a distress alert relay on HF and the vessel in distress is probably in close proximity.

URGENCY CALL

Vessels receiving a DSC urgency call should:

- COMMENCE LOG KEEPING AND INFORM THE MASTER
- SET WATCH ON THE INDICATED CHANNEL OR FREQUENCY
- IF A MESSAGE IS HEARD, RESPOND BY RADIOTELEPHONY IF APPROPRIATE. OTHERWISE, LISTEN FOR FIVE MINUTES
- IF NO MESSAGE OR WORKING IS HEARD, CONTACT A SHORE STATION.
- CONTINUE ROUTINE WORKING

SAFETY CALL

Vessels receiving a DSC safety call should not acknowledge receipt but listen to the channel or frequency indicated for the safety message. Again, this is what happened in the past with radiotelephony communications. You would not have acknowledged a call from Niton Radio inviting all ships to listen to the navigational warnings.

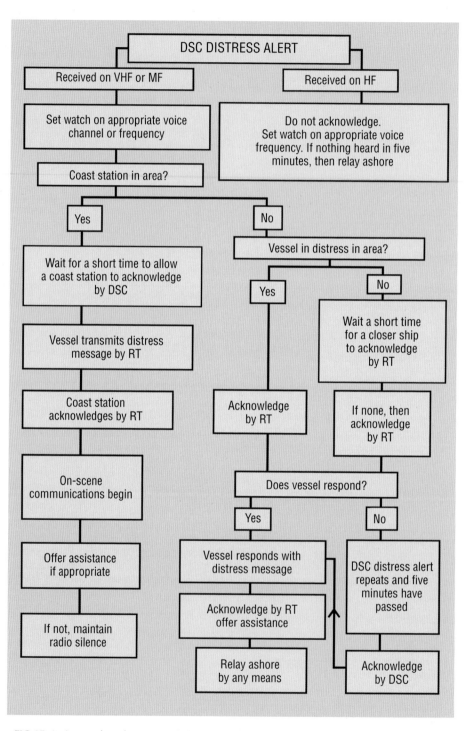

FIG 15 Actions to be taken on receiving a DSC distress alert.

ROUTINE CALL

If a vessel receives an individual routine call from another vessel or coast station, a DSC acknowledgement should be transmitted indicating whether the vessel is able to communicate as requested. The receipt of an individual routine DSC call is the only time a DSC acknowledgement is always sent. If a coast station is unable to accept the ship's traffic immediately it is the responsibility of the ship to make contact later. In ship to ship communications the called ship would make contact at a later time if it was not able to accept traffic immediately.

DSC PRIORITIES/CALL CATEGORIES

The distress button is only used for 'own ship' distress situations.
    The options on a Class A controller are:

- DISTRESS
- DISTRESS RELAY
- ALL SHIPS URGENCY (VHF only, on new equipment)
- ALL SHIPS SAFETY (VHF only, on new equipment)
- INDIVIDUAL
- GROUP
- GEOGRAPHIC AREA (For urgency and safety on new MF/HF equipment)
- TELEPHONE

The options on a Class D controller are:

- DISTRESS
- ALL SHIPS URGENCY
- ALL SHIPS SAFETY
- INDIVIDUAL with intership working channel options 06, 08, 72 and 77.

With a Class D controller, the channel 70 receiver is not required to operate when the transmitter is in use. Only one antenna is required. Any alerts that occur whilst the transmitter is in use will not, therefore, be recorded. If an alert is received, then the DSC controller will automatically switch the transceiver to the working channel identified within the incoming transmission.

    It is important to remember the specific DSC priorities. For instance, if you were asked which call category you would use on behalf of another vessel in distress, the answer would be 'distress relay'. Answering 'mayday relay' would be incorrect because that signal is relevant to radiotelephony communications, not DSC.

    Any category of DSC announcement that is received by the controller will automatically be stored in the unit's log. The capacity of the log will differ from unit to unit.

Small craft GMDSS class D VHF DSC.

CLASSES OF DSC CONTROLLER

Each class of controller will have different functions. The Class A controller is the most sophisticated as it will enable geographic area calls and automatic telephone calls without the intervention of an operator. The Class A controller is the type that will most often be installed on compulsorily fitted vessels. The VHF Class D and MF/HF Class E controllers have been produced for the leisure market, fishing and other non-SOLAS regulated vessels. Alerting for own ship distress is possible, in addition to urgency, safety and routine calling to an individual station or a group of stations.

CANCELLING FALSE ALERTS

If a DSC distress alert is sent in error, it is important to cancel it. The rescue authorities could waste much valuable time and lives could unnecessarily be put at risk if an operator fails to do this. Let the alert finish and stop it from repeating by switching the unit off or pressing the cancel button. Tune the transceiver to the channel or frequency advised in the alert – this may already have been done automatically by the controller. Make a transmission to all stations cancelling the false alert and include your MMSI number. If an operator has been careless enough to send a multi-frequency distress alert in error, he or she is going to be busy as transmissions will have to be made in each band.

An example of a transmission made to cancel a false alert:

```
ALL STATIONS x 3
THIS IS
NAME x 3
CALLSIGN x 1
MMSI x 1
CANCEL MY DISTRESS ALERT (OF TIME IN UTC)
OUT
```

AVOIDING FALSE ALERTS

It is far better, for all concerned, to avoid sending false alerts. Ensure that all crew members likely to use the equipment on board have been instructed in its correct use. With modern equipment it is difficult to send an alert in error because of the spring-loaded cover on the distress button and the requirement to hold the button in for three or five seconds. The older types of equipment were not as well designed and it was easier to send a distress alert in error. Our world has become very automated and many of us have developed a habit of random button pushing in preference to reading the instruction manual. This must not be permitted. If the unit has any complicated functions, display the instructions on the bulkhead if necessary. One of the people nominated in the GMDSS log book should carry out the daily and weekly tests and ensure that false alerts are not generated during the testing procedure. If the ship changes hands, ensure that the registration of the MMSI is updated and, if necessary, that the unit is reprogrammed.

Questions

1 What is the minimum amount of information that can be included in a DSC distress alert?

2 What is a distress alert called that includes the minimum amount of information?

3 If the nature of the distress is included, what is this type of alert?

4 If you are in an A3 area and receive a DSC distress alert on 2187.5 kHz, what is the procedure that you should follow?

5 If you are in an A1 area and receive a DSC distress alert on channel 70, what is the procedure that you should follow?

6 If you are in an A3 area and receive a DSC distress alert on channel 70, what is the procedure that you should follow?

Questions

7 If you receive a DSC distress alert on 8414.5 kHz, what is the procedure that you should follow?

8 If you receive a DSC distress alert relay from a coast station on HF, directed to all ships in a geographic area, what is the procedure that you should follow?

9 If you receive a DSC urgency call addressed to all ships or a geographic area, what is the procedure that you should follow?

10 Which DSC priority or call category would you select if you had:

a) A distress situation on board your own vessel?

b) A medical emergency on board and needed assistance from nearby ships?

c) A medical emergency on board and needed advice from a doctor?

d) To obtain assistance on behalf of a vessel that was in distress?

e) Sighted a floating container that was a hazard to navigation?

11 What action would you take if you sent a DSC distress alert in error?

MF/HF DSC combined unit.

Answers

1 The minimum amount of information that can be included in a DSC distress alert is the vessel's MMSI, the position and the time that the position was valid.

2 A DSC distress alert that includes the minimum amount of information is called undesignated.

3 If the nature of the distress is included, the alert is designated.

4 If you are in an A3 area and receive a DSC distress alert on 2187.5 kHz, you should commence log keeping and inform the Master. Set watch on 2182 kHz (or 2174.5 kHz for telex working). Acknowledge by radiotelephony. If there is no response to your radiotelephony acknowledgement, no working is heard, the alert repeats and five minutes have passed, acknowledge by DSC and relay the information ashore by any means.

5 If you are in an A1 area and receive a DSC distress alert on channel 70, you should commence log keeping and inform the Master. Set watch on channel 16. Wait a short time for a coast station to acknowledge. If they do not, acknowledge by radiotelephony. If there is no response to your radiotelephony acknowledgement and no working is heard, relay the information ashore by any means. To avoid congestion of channel 70 in an A1 area, it is not advisable to acknowledge by DSC, unless the alert keeps repeating.

6 If you are in an A3 area and receive a DSC distress alert on channel 70, you should commence log keeping and inform the Master. Set watch on channel 16. Acknowledge by radiotelephony immediately. If there is no response to your radiotelephony acknowledgement, no working is heard, the alert repeats and five minutes have passed, acknowledge by DSC and relay the information ashore by any means.

Answers

7 If you receive a DSC distress alert on 8414.5 kHz, you should not acknowledge. You should commence log keeping and inform the Master. Set watch on 8291 kHz or the appropriate telex frequency. Listen for five minutes and if no working is heard, relay the information ashore by any means.

8 If you receive a distress alert relay from a coast station on HF addressed to all ships within a geographic area, you should acknowledge by radiotelephony on the appropriate frequency in the same band.

9 If you receive a DSC urgency call, you should set watch on the indicated channel or frequency. If a message is heard, respond by radiotelephony if appropriate, otherwise listen for five minutes and if no message or working is heard, contact a shore station and continue routine working.

10 a) Distress alert would be selected for distress situations on board your own vessel.

b) All ships urgency by VHF or geographic area urgency by MF would be selected to obtain assistance from nearby vessels.

c) Individual urgency would be selected to obtain medical advice from a doctor.

d) Distress relay would be selected to obtain assistance on behalf of another vessel that was in distress.

e) All ships safety by VHF or geographic area safety by MF would be selected if you had sighted a floating container.

11 If a DSC distress alert is sent in error, it is important to cancel it. Let the alert finish and stop it from repeating by switching the unit off or pressing the cancel button. Tune the transceiver to the radiotelephony channel or frequency advised in the alert. Make a broadcast to all stations cancelling the false alert and include your MMSI.

6 DSC and Radiotelephony Procedures

We have seen in Chapter 5 that DSC is a digital alerting and calling system that operates on VHF, MF and HF. The system provides for distress alerting, urgency, safety and routine calling, the equivalent to Mayday, Pan Pan, Sécurité and routine calling by radiotelephony. It is important to be clear in your mind which system you are using, especially with combined units.

DISTRESS

Distress has priority over all other communications. A distress alert should only be sent on the authority of the Master or the Captain of the vessel when there is grave and imminent danger requiring immediate assistance. A vessel receiving a distress alert should immediately cease all transmissions likely to interfere with distress working and listen. Any vessel receiving a distress signal from another vessel is duty bound to act upon it. This action may be to render assistance or, if another station is handling the situation, to simply keep quiet. The definition of distress changed with the implementation of GMDSS to include serious and imminent danger to life. Students should learn that the use of a distress alert indicates that A MOBILE UNIT (SHIP, AIRCRAFT OR OTHER VEHICLE) OR A PERSON IS THREATENED BY GRAVE AND IMMINENT DANGER AND REQUIRES IMMEDIATE ASSISTANCE.

The first action of a vessel in distress is to send a DSC distress alert on an appropriate channel or frequency. In area A1, channel 70 would be used and in area A2, 2187.5 kHz. In areas A3 and A4, 2187.5 kHz would be used to alert nearby shipping and an appropriate HF frequency would be used to alert a coast station if the HF equipment option has been taken; 8414.5 kHz would be a good first choice if there was not enough time to work out propagation paths.

If you have a fast-moving situation, the regulations do allow the transmission of a distress call and message immediately following a distress alert, in order to attract attention from as many ships as possible. However, it is more common to wait for a DSC acknowledgement from a coast station and monitor the appropriate radiotelephony frequency for an acknowledgement from a ship. If the DSC controller is not being updated with position information from GPS, work out a position for the distress message that will shortly follow.

On receipt of one or more acknowledgements, the vessel in distress transmits its distress call and message by radiotelephony. The distress call should be spoken to attract the attention of those craft not yet fitted with DSC equipment.

Distress Call

The distress call is a broadcast, which means that it is not addressed to any station:

MAYDAY x 3

THIS IS

NAME x 3

CALLSIGN x 1

MMSI x 1

Distress Message

Without waiting for a response, continue with the distress message:

M MAYDAY

I IDENTIFICATION – NAME, CALLSIGN AND MMSI

P POSITION

N NATURE OF THE DISTRESS

A ASSISTANCE REQUIRED

N NUMBER ON BOARD

O OTHER INFORMATION

O OVER

The mnemonic MIPNANOO can be used for distress messages and should be learnt by all students. It may also be used for urgency and safety messages in a slightly modified format:

M The distress signal is the single word MAYDAY from the French *m'aidez*, meaning 'help me', and should prefix all transmissions during distress working in order to keep the radio silence in force.

I The vessel's identifications are listed here. Name, callsign and MMSI must be included.

P The position comes next and is the most important piece of information in the message. It may differ from the DSC position if GPS has failed and the position has been entered manually, and is therefore old. The DSC controller can only display a latitude and longitude. If there is a charted object in sight, use it as a reference in the radiotelephony message because a range and bearing is far more tangible than a latitude and longitude. The bearing must always be from the object of reference out to sea. If using a hand bearing compass to gain a bearing, the reciprocal is calculated by adding 180 to a figure less than 180 or subtracting 180 from a figure greater than 180. For example, the reciprocal bearing of 270°, or due West, is 090° or due East. When speaking these bearings, always use three figures and speak the numbers individually. For example, 5° would be spoken as zero zero five degrees. This way, there is no ambiguity.

N The nature of the distress should be as brief as possible. 'Sinking' is fine, there is no need to transmit the unfortunate circumstances that lead to the situation. Remember that hopefully someone is trying to write your message in a log book.

A The type of assistance required will usually just be spoken as 'require immediate assistance'. However, if there is something specific that will help, by all means include it here.

N The number of persons on board is needed to plan the resources that are to be used for the rescue. There is little point in sending a RIB to save 200 crew. In cold waters, where casualties may be suffering from hypothermia, it is wise to advise the numbers in advance.

O Any other information that may assist the rescue should be included. Perhaps the visibility is poor or perhaps there are some distinguishing features that might help identify the vessel.

O The word 'over' indicates the end of your message and invites a reply.

A coast station will hopefully acknowledge the distress message in the following manner:

MAYDAY
IDENTIFICATION OF VESSEL IN DISTRESS x 3
THIS IS
COAST STATION x 3
RECEIVED MAYDAY
OVER

If no coast station has heard the transmission, ships may acknowledge in the same manner, after which the rescue will start to be co-ordinated. Callsigns are always spoken three times when working distress. The procedural words 'Received Mayday' must be in that order, so think 'I have received your Mayday' and you will be correct.

If the above distress procedure is followed and no response is heard, check the equipment to ensure that all of the controls are properly set. For example, if using VHF, ensure that dual watch has been turned off, that the squelch is correctly set, that high power has been selected and that the PTT switch that was depressed for transmission is released for reception. Try again, and if there is no response try another frequency or channel and then any other means that are available to you.

ON-SCENE COMMUNICATIONS

On-scene communications are those between the vessel in distress and other stations assisting in the rescue. On a local scale there are numerous Coastguard stations around the UK that deal with situations daily. On a wider scale, Maritime Rescue Co-ordination Centres (MRCC) have been put in place specifically to co-ordinate Search And Rescue (SAR) operations. Coast stations (terrestrial), land earth stations (INMARSAT) and local user terminals (COSPAS/SARSAT EPIRB) will all link via various routes to the MRCC. (See figure 1, page 12.) Simplex radiotelephony is the preferred method of communication, on channel 16 (156.8 MHz) and 2182 kHz. In addition, 3023 kHz and the primary VHF intership channel 06 may also be used for aeronautical SAR. Until informed otherwise, all stations not taking part in the rescue should assist by maintaining radio silence on the frequency handling distress working.

PROCEDURAL WORDS RELATING TO DISTRESS WORKING

If at any time during distress working the controlling station wishes to impose radio silence on an interfering station, the procedural words 'seelonce mayday' would be used. The controlling station can be a coast station, the vessel in distress, a relay vessel or an on-scene co-ordinator. The words may be included as part of the following transmission:

```
MAYDAY
ALL STATIONS x 3
THIS IS
NAME x 3
CALLSIGN x 1
SEELONCE MAYDAY
OUT
```

The end of distress working is indicated by the words 'seelonce feenee', the silence has finished and normal working may commence. The procedural words may be included as part of the following transmission:

```
MAYDAY
ALL STATIONS x 3
THIS IS
NAME x 3
CALLSIGN x 1
TIME (IN UTC) OF HANDING IN MESSAGE
NAME CALLSIGN MMSI OF THE VESSEL IN DISTRESS
SEELONCE FEENEE
OUT
```

DISTRESS RELAY

When a station learns that another vessel is in distress it may transmit a distress relay alert on its behalf, if:

- Having received a distress alert, it is not acknowledged by a coast station or another vessel within five minutes.
- The vessel in distress cannot transmit the distress alert itself.
- The master of a vessel not itself in distress, or an MRCC, considers that further assistance is required.

It is imperative to make it clear that it is not your vessel that is in distress but that you are the relay vessel. This option is selected from the list of priorities in the DSC controller. In the first instance, a DSC distress relay alert should preferably be addressed to a coast station. The coast station will then appoint somebody as on-scene co-ordinator, if it cannot perform the role itself. The co-ordinator would then send the DSC distress relay alert to all ships in the area.

If a DSC distress alert is received from a ship, a DSC distress alert relay should not be sent to all ships, unless it is clear that nobody else received it.

Next the distress relay call and message will be transmitted. The call must be addressed either to an individual coast station or to all stations. This would match the DSC alert that was sent previously.

Mayday relay call

MAYDAY RELAY x 3
COAST STATION x 3 **OR** ALL STATIONS x 3
THIS IS
NAME of relay station x 3
CALLSIGN of relay station x 1
MMSI of relay station x 1

Mayday relay message

Without waiting for a response, continue with the mayday relay message:

M MAYDAY
I IDENTIFICATION – NAME, CALLSIGN AND MMSI of the vessel in distress, if unknown use UNIDENTIFIED (TYPE OF VESSEL)
P POSITION – of the vessel in distress
N NATURE OF THE DISTRESS
A ASSISTANCE REQUIRED
N NUMBER ON BOARD – if known
O OTHER INFORMATION
O OVER

URGENCY

Urgency takes priority over all communications other than distress. An urgency call should only be sent on the authority of the Master or the Captain of the vessel. Students should know that the urgency signal indicates that A VERY URGENT MESSAGE CONCERNING THE SAFETY OF A MOBILE UNIT OR A PERSON is to follow. The urgency signal is PAN PAN from the French *une panne*, which means a breakdown. The signal may prefix urgent situations, including a breakdown, the report of a vessel that is overdue, or a medical problem.

The announcement is by a DSC urgency call on an appropriate channel or frequency. Frequencies used for urgency are the same as those used for distress. The DSC urgency call may be addressed to all ships on VHF, a geographic area on MF or HF, a group of ships or an individual station. Wait for a DSC acknowledgement from a coast station. Ships do not have the facility to acknowledge by DSC. Next, GMDSS regulations require the vessel to transmit the urgency call and message by radiotelephony. The call should be spoken to attract the attention of those craft not yet fitted with DSC equipment. The call must be addressed to either an individual station or to all stations, since it is not a broadcast.

Urgency call

PAN PAN x 3

ALL STATIONS x 3 **OR** INDIVIDUAL STATION x 3

THIS IS

NAME x 3

CALLSIGN x 1

MMSI x 1

Urgency message

Without waiting for a response, continue with the urgency message:

P PAN PAN

I IDENTIFICATION – NAME, CALLSIGN AND MMSI

P POSITION

N NATURE OF THE URGENCY

A ASSISTANCE REQUIRED
(Require urgent assistance is used if nothing specific is required)

N NUMBER ON BOARD (May or may not be relevant)

O OTHER INFORMATION

O OVER

GMDSS console for a large ship.

SAFETY

Safety takes priority over all communications other than distress and urgency. The safety signal is SÉCURITÉ from the French *la sécurité*, meaning 'the safety'. Its use indicates that THE CALLING STATION HAS AN IMPORTANT NAVIGATIONAL OR METEOROLOGICAL WARNING TO TRANSMIT.

The announcement is by a DSC safety call on an appropriate channel or frequency. The frequencies are the same as those used for distress and urgency. The DSC safety call may be addressed to all ships on VHF, a geographic area on MF or HF, a group of ships or an individual ship and should include the channel or frequency for the radiotelephony message. A DSC announcement is not required prior to a timetabled broadcast. The radiotelephony safety call will be transmitted on channel 16 or 2182 kHz to attract the attention of those craft not yet fitted with DSC equipment. Remember that the call should be addressed to either an individual station or, more often, to all stations and include the channel or frequency for the message.

Safety call

SÉCURITÉ x 3

ALL STATIONS x 3

THIS IS

NAME x 3

CALLSIGN x 1

MMSI x 1

LISTEN CHANNEL 06 FOR MY NAVIGATION WARNING

OUT

Safety message will follow on the working channel or frequency, where the call will also be repeated.

SÉCURITÉ x 3

ALL STATIONS x 3

THIS IS

NAME x 3

CALLSIGN x 1

MMSI x 1

Without waiting for a response, continue with the safety message:

S SÉCURITÉ

I IDENTIFICATION – NAME, CALLSIGN AND MMSI
   NAVIGATION WARNING AT 1400 UTC

P POSITION

N NATURE OF THE SAFETY MESSAGE

A ADVICE

O OTHER INFORMATION

O OUT

ROUTINE PROCEDURES

VHF channel 70 is used for distress, urgency, safety and routine transmissions by DSC. Separate announcing frequencies are used for public correspondence in the MF and HF bands. If a ship is calling a coast radio station of the same flag, national DSC frequencies can be found in ALRS/ADRS Volume 1. The international MF DSC frequency for public correspondence may be used between ships and coast stations of different nationality: the ship transmits to the coast station on 2189.5 kHz; the coast station transmits to the ship on 2177 kHz. The frequency 2177 kHz is also used for DSC routine calling between ships.

This arrangement can be confusing. However, if 2177 kHz is monitored, the station will receive routine calls from other ships as well as calls from coast stations. If no acknowledgement is received in five minutes, the call may be repeated. Further attempts should be transmitted at 15-minute intervals.

Details of calling arrangements for coast stations will be found in ALRS/ADRS Volume 1. Ports and marinas have always been called direct on working channels and little is expected to change. If large ports decide to monitor for DSC calls, details will be found in ALRS/ADRS Volume 6. UK Coastguard stations have been allocated MMSI numbers and have area A1 DSC equipment. Details can be found in ALRS/ADRS Volume 5, or Volume 1. Some UK Coastguard stations will also be monitoring 2187.5 kHz. Skippers of small craft are not required to carry ALRS/ADRS and will find all relevant information in one of the nautical almanacs.

CONTACTING A VESSEL WHOSE MMSI IS UNKNOWN

If you are about to be run down by a ship, a DSC distress alert could be used. However, the likelihood of the ship identifying itself from this alert is uncertain. If the ship is further off and you think that a risk of collision exists, a DSC urgency call could be used. If you know the name of the ship, a radiotelephony call on channel 16 or 13 could help you make contact.

However, it is never advisable to use radio communications for collision avoidance due to the notoriously poor success rate. It is far better to take early action to avoid these situations.

The main difficulty may come when you wish to contact another vessel for routine communications but you do not know the MMSI number and you do not carry the means to look it up. Routine calling by radiotelephony may be conducted on channel 16 and 2182 kHz until advised otherwise.

Most modern equipment will not permit radiotelephony communications on the dedicated DSC channel or frequencies. However, many transceivers in use were manufactured before the implementation of GMDSS standards. It is important to ensure that radiotelephony is never transmitted on the dedicated DSC channel or frequencies. The DSC receivers will not recognise radiotelephony transmissions and this action could interfere with a digital distress alert.

DSC announcements – To help you remember					
	DSC ALERT	DSC CALL	Addressed to a GEOGRAPHIC AREA	Addressed to ALL SHIPS	Addressed to an INDIVIDUAL STATION
DISTRESS VHF					
DISTRESS MF/HF					
DISTRESS RELAY VHF					
DISTRESS RELAY MF					
DISTRESS RELAY HF					
URGENCY VHF					
URGENCY MF					
URGENCY HF					
SAFETY VHF					
SAFETY MF					
SAFETY HF					

Questions

1 Put the following transmissions into their correct order of priority and explain why.

a) A cyclone warning

b) Ship movements

c) To report sighting of red flares

d) A request for medical advice

2 What does the use of the distress priority indicate?

3 If you send a DSC distress alert on channel 70 in an A1 area and receive no DSC acknowledgement, what should you do?

4 Give an example of a distress call on 2182 kHz and state when it would be used.

5 You are in an A1 area. Your vessel's name is Midnight Blue, callsign MRWA3, MMSI 232123456. You have struck a submerged object and are sinking. St Catherine's Light bears 350° from you and you are six miles off. You have six people on board and an EPIRB. State the full GMDSS procedure that you should follow, including the radiotelephony transmission that you should make and the channels that you should use.

6 If a coast station received the above distress transmission, how should they acknowledge it by radiotelephony?

7 Name the channel that can be used for international aeronautical SAR.

8 If a controlling station wishes to impose radio silence on an interfering station during distress working, which procedural words would be used?

9 What is meant by the words seelonce feenee?

10 A light aircraft has ditched just off your port bow. You are in position 51° 44´ N 007° 23´ W within area A2 and sea conditions are rough. Your vessel's name is White Tiger, callsign GRWQ9, MMSI 232456789. State the procedure that you should follow, including the radiotelephony transmission that you should make and the frequencies that you should use to relay this ashore.

11 What does the use of the urgency signal indicate?

12 You are in an A1 area, your vessel's name is Warrior, callsign MJDS4, MMSI 233123457, and you are a 1500 GRT ship. You have lost your propeller and require a tow. You are in a position where Nab Tower bears 340° and you are five miles off. State the full GMDSS procedure that you should follow, including the radiotelephony transmission that you should make and the channels that you should use.

13 What does the use of the safety signal indicate?

Questions

14 You are in an A3 area, it is 1800 UTC, your vessel's name is Sarpedon, callsign MGME8, MMSI 234234556. You have sighted a floating metal container that is a hazard to navigation in position 47° 34´ N 013° 54´ W. Shipping in close proximity needs to be warned to keep a lookout. State the full GMDSS procedure that you should follow, including the radiotelephony transmission that you should make and the channels you should use.

15 Which radiotelephony signal would you associate with the following DSC priorities/call categories?

a) Distress

b) Distress relay

c) Urgency

d) Safety

16 Which VHF channel would be used to send a routine DSC call?

17 There is an international DSC frequency for public correspondence that may be used between a ship and a coast station of different nationality. On which frequency would the ship call the coast station and on which frequency would the coast station reply?

18 What is the MF DSC frequency for routine ship to ship calls?

Answers

1 The correct order of priority would be:

c) To report sighting of red flares – Distress relay

d) A request for medical advice – Urgency

a) A cyclone warning – Safety

b) Ship movements – Port operations

2 The use of the distress priority indicates that a mobile unit (ship, aircraft or other vehicle) or a person is threatened by grave and imminent danger and requires immediate assistance.

3 If you send a DSC distress alert on channel 70 in an A1 area and receive no DSC acknowledgement after a short while, you should broadcast your distress call and message on channel 16.

4 A distress call on 2182 kHz would be used to prefix a distress message. The call is: Mayday x 3, this is, name x 3, callsign x 1, MMSI x 1.

5 The announcement is by a DSC distress alert on channel 70, followed by a radiotelephony call and message on channel 16:

Mayday x 3

This is

Midnight Blue x 3

MRWA3 x 1

232123456 x 1

Mayday

Midnight Blue, MRWA3, MMSI 232123456

170° from St Catherine's Light, six miles

Sinking

Require immediate assistance

Six persons on board

EPIRB activated

Over

6 The above distress transmission would be acknowledged by radiotelephony on channel 16 in the following way:

Mayday

Midnight Blue x 3

This is

Coast station x 3

Received mayday

Over

Answers

7 The channel that can be used for international aeronautical SAR is VHF channel 06.

8 If a controlling station wishes to impose radio silence on an interfering station during distress working, seelonce mayday would be used.

9 Seelonce feenee is used to indicate that distress working has finished and normal working may resume.

10 The announcement is by a DSC distress relay alert to a shore station on 2187.5 kHz, followed by the call and message on 2182 kHz.

Mayday Relay x 3
Coast Station x 3
This is
White Tiger x 3
GRWQ9 x 1
232456789 x 1

Mayday
Unidentified light aircraft
51° 44′ N 007° 23′ W
Ditched in sea
Requires immediate assistance
Sea conditions are rough
Over

11 The urgency signal indicates that a very urgent message is to follow concerning the safety of a mobile unit or a person.

12 The announcement is by a DSC all ships urgency call on channel 70, followed by an urgency call and message by radiotelephony on channel 16.

Pan Pan x 3
All Stations x 3
This is
Warrior x 3
MJDS4 x 1
233123457 x 1

Pan Pan
Warrior, MJDS4, 233123457
Nab Tower bears 160°, five miles
Propeller lost
Require a tow
We are a 1500 GRT ship
Over

Answers

13 Use of the safety signal indicates that the calling station has an important navigational or meteorological warning to transmit.

14 The announcement is by a DSC all ships safety call on channel 70, indicating channel 06 for the message, followed by the radiotelephony call on channel 16. The call and message would follow on a working channel.

Sécurité x 3
All Stations x 3
This is
Sarpedon x 3
MGME8 x 1
234234556 x 1
Listen channel 06 for my navigation warning
Out

On channel 06

Sécurité x 3
All Stations x 3
This is
Sarpedon x 3
MGME8 x 1
234234556 x 1

Sécurité
Sarpedon, MGME8, 234234556
Navigation warning at 1800 UTC
47° 34′ N 013° 54′ W
Floating metal container sighted, danger to navigation
Vessels advised to keep a lookout
Out

15 The radiotelephony signals associated with the following DSC priorities/call categories are:

a) Distress – Mayday

b) Distress relay – Mayday relay

c) Urgency – Pan Pan

d) Safety – Sécurité

16 VHF channel 70 would be used to send a routine DSC call.

17 The ship would send a routine DSC call to the coast station on 2189.5 kHz. The coast station would reply on 2177 kHz.

18 The MF DSC frequency for routine ship to ship calls is 2177 kHz.

7 The Radiotelephony Examination

This chapter is primarily for the ROC, LRC and GOC candidates. However, the radiotelephony procedures that are included are relevant to anyone involved in maritime communications.

Procedures and log-keeping ability are tested during the radiotelephony examination. Marks will be lost for incorrect procedure. For example, the use of incorrect phonetics, acknowledging a distress message with 'Mayday Received' instead of 'Received Mayday' or forgetting to prefix every transmission during distress working with the signal 'Mayday'.

The radio log is a legal document that must be completed correctly, in ink. Each time daily, weekly and monthly tests are logged, the operator who conducted the tests must sign his or her name against the entry. When an operator goes on and off radio watch an entry should also be made to that effect with a signature against it. If a mistake is made, simply put a single line through the entry and initial it. Do not leave any blank lines and remember to use UTC for time keeping.

At the start of the examination you will be given a sheet of paper showing details of your vessel and informing you which sea area you are in and whether or not to expect coast station involvement. These details will include the vessel's name, position, callsign and MMSI. The additional information is for use when reporting your vessel's position and ETA (see Figure 16 below and Figure 17, page 74). Blank log pages will also be provided.

The easiest way of explaining this exercise is to run a scenario. This example is of distress working. Only two ships will be used as this is enough to demonstrate the procedures. However, in practice, a group of eight students would normally be examined together. The specimen log at the end of the chapter, Figure 19, is from the vessel *Sarpedon*.

Name of ship SARPEDON
Position 19° 51′N 040° 04′W

Callsign MGME8
MMSI 232181956

ADDITIONAL INFORMATION
You are 10 miles from the incident bearing 180° speed 20 knots
ETA 30 minutes

FIG 16 Exercise details for the vessel *Sarpedon*.

```
Name of ship ARGENT              Callsign MPLA6
Position 20° 06′N 040° 09′W      MMSI 233257683

            ADDITIONAL INFORMATION
You are 6 miles from the incident bearing 315° speed 8 knots
                 ETA 45 minutes
```

FIG 17 Exercise details for the vessel *Argent*.

When you are told to start, enter details of your vessel at the top of the page. Then enter the date and the time that you would have carried out your daily tests. Log the entry numbered 1 in the sample log – this will include the ship's position, time it was valid and details of the daily checks – and sign your name against it.

Next, the examiner will give you details of a DSC alert which has been received on your bridge (see Figure 18).

```
        DSC DISTRESS ALERT RECEIVED ON 2187.5 kHz

                    212445089
                20° 01′N 040° 01′W
                    1030 UTC
                    SINKING
                      J3E
```

FIG 18 Details of the received DSC distress alert.

Log the DSC distress alert as in entry number 2, taking care to copy down the vessel's position accurately. If either of the distress positions is wrong, you automatically fail this examination. The alert gives a position and time. Remember that this is the time that the position was valid and not necessarily the time that you received the alert. Use the clock for that information eg 1100 UTC. If the GPS has failed, the position could have been entered manually and be old, as in this example.

Until the DSC distress alert was received, your DSC controller was keeping watch for you on the DSC distress frequencies while you went about your normal business. The DSC will continue to do this. You should now sign yourself on watch on 2182 kHz. This is the entry numbered 3 in the sample log.

Entry number 4 in this example is the distress call and message. The call is logged by an entry in the 'to' and 'from' columns; the message is logged in full in the 'summary of communications' column.

The transmission from the vessel in distress would be as follows:

MAYDAY, MAYDAY, MAYDAY
THIS IS
MARTHA, MARTHA, MARTHA,
CALLSIGN DELTA HOTEL ALPHA LIMA
MMSI TWO ONE TWO FOUR FOUR FIVE
ZERO EIGHT NINE

MAYDAY
MARTHA (often spelt phonetically)
CALLSIGN DELTA HOTEL ALPHA LIMA
MMSI TWO ONE TWO FOUR FOUR FIVE
ZERO EIGHT NINE
IN POSITION TWO ZERO DEGREES ZERO
TWO MINUTES NORTH ZERO FOUR ZERO
DEGREES ZERO FIVE MINUTES WEST
I SAY AGAIN MY POSITION
TWO ZERO DEGREES ZERO TWO
MINUTES NORTH ZERO FOUR ZERO
DEGREES ZERO FIVE MINUTES WEST
SINKING
REQUIRE IMMEDIATE ASSISTANCE
ONE FIVE PERSONS ON BOARD
THREE ZERO ZERO METRES VISIBILITY
OVER

Each vessel in turn will then acknowledge the distress message by radiotelephony, following the appropriate procedure. Each transmission should start with the signal 'Mayday' and callsigns are repeated three times. After each acknowledgement in this example, the vessel in distress indicates that the transmission has been received. To make log keeping easier, log both transmissions on the same line. This is entry number 5. R Mayday, or R SOS, may be used as an abbreviation for 'received mayday' and SB as an abbreviation for 'stand by', indicating the response from the vessel in distress:

MAYDAY
DELTA HOTEL ALPHA LIMA
DELTA HOTEL ALPHA LIMA
DELTA HOTEL ALPHA LIMA
THIS IS
MIKE GOLF MIKE ECHO EIGHT

MIKE GOLF MIKE ECHO EIGHT
MIKE GOLF MIKE ECHO EIGHT
RECEIVED MAYDAY
VESSEL'S NAME SARPEDON, I SPELL, SIERRA ALPHA ROMEO PAPA
ECHO DELTA OSCAR NOVEMBER
OVER

The vessel in distress replies:

MAYDAY
MIKE GOLF MIKE ECHO EIGHT
MIKE GOLF MIKE ECHO EIGHT
MIKE GOLF MIKE ECHO EIGHT
THIS IS
DELTA HOTEL ALPHA LIMA
DELTA HOTEL ALPHA LIMA
DELTA HOTEL ALPHA LIMA
RECEIVED
STAND BY

MAYDAY
DELTA HOTEL ALPHA LIMA
DELTA HOTEL ALPHA LIMA
DELTA HOTEL ALPHA LIMA
THIS IS
MIKE PAPA LIMA ALPHA SIX
MIKE PAPA LIMA ALPHA SIX
MIKE PAPA LIMA ALPHA SIX
RECEIVED MAYDAY
VESSEL'S NAME ARGENT, I SPELL ALPHA ROMEO GOLF ECHO
NOVEMBER TANGO
OVER

The vessel in distress replies:

MAYDAY
MIKE PAPA LIMA ALPHA SIX
MIKE PAPA LIMA ALPHA SIX
MIKE PAPA LIMA ALPHA SIX
THIS IS
DELTA HOTEL ALPHA LIMA
DELTA HOTEL ALPHA LIMA
DELTA HOTEL ALPHA LIMA
RECEIVED
STAND BY

On completion of all acknowledgements in this example, the vessel in distress will call each vessel in turn requesting its position and ETA. This may be logged as 'Pos?' These entries may also be logged on one line. This is entry number 6. However, you will see that the callsigns have now changed columns as the vessel in distress initiated the communications. When responding, individual figures should be used and the information should be repeated using the procedural words 'I say again'. Do not forget to log your own entry.

> MAYDAY
> MIKE GOLF MIKE ECHO EIGHT
> MIKE GOLF MIKE ECHO EIGHT
> MIKE GOLF MIKE ECHO EIGHT
> THIS IS
> DELTA HOTEL ALPHA LIMA
> DELTA HOTEL ALPHA LIMA
> DELTA HOTEL ALPHA LIMA
> REPORT YOUR POSITION AND ETA
> OVER

MAYDAY
DELTA HOTEL ALPHA LIMA
DELTA HOTEL ALPHA LIMA
DELTA HOTEL ALPHA LIMA
THIS IS
MIKE GOLF MIKE ECHO EIGHT
MIKE GOLF MIKE ECHO EIGHT
MIKE GOLF MIKE ECHO EIGHT
MY POSITION ONE ZERO MILES BEARING ONE EIGHT ZERO
DEGREES FROM YOU
SPEED TWO ZERO KNOTS
ETA THREE ZERO MINUTES
I SAY AGAIN
MY POSITION ONE ZERO MILES BEARING ONE EIGHT ZERO
DEGREES FROM YOU
SPEED TWO ZERO KNOTS
ETA THREE ZERO MINUTES
OVER

The vessel in distress replies, and may ask you to stand by or proceed:

> MAYDAY
> MIKE GOLF MIKE ECHO EIGHT
> MIKE GOLF MIKE ECHO EIGHT
> MIKE GOLF MIKE ECHO EIGHT
> THIS IS

DELTA HOTEL ALPHA LIMA
DELTA HOTEL ALPHA LIMA
DELTA HOTEL ALPHA LIMA
ALL RECEIVED STAND BY

MAYDAY
MIKE PAPA LIMA ALPHA SIX
MIKE PAPA LIMA ALPHA SIX
MIKE PAPA LIMA ALPHA SIX
THIS IS
DELTA HOTEL ALPHA LIMA
DELTA HOTEL ALPHA LIMA
DELTA HOTEL ALPHA LIMA
REPORT YOUR POSITION AND ETA
OVER

MAYDAY
DELTA HOTEL ALPHA LIMA
DELTA HOTEL ALPHA LIMA
DELTA HOTEL ALPHA LIMA
THIS IS
MIKE PAPA LIMA ALPHA SIX
MIKE PAPA LIMA ALPHA SIX
MIKE PAPA LIMA ALPHA SIX
MY POSITION SIX MILES BEARING THREE ONE
FIVE DEGREES FROM YOU
SPEED EIGHT KNOTS
ETA FOUR FIVE MINUTES
I SAY AGAIN
MY POSITION SIX MILES BEARING THREE ONE
FIVE DEGREES FROM YOU
SPEED EIGHT KNOTS
ETA FOUR FIVE MINUTES
OVER

The vessel in distress replies:

MAYDAY
MIKE PAPA LIMA ALPHA SIX
MIKE PAPA LIMA ALPHA SIX
MIKE PAPA LIMA ALPHA SIX
THIS IS
DELTA HOTEL ALPHA LIMA
DELTA HOTEL ALPHA LIMA
DELTA HOTEL ALPHA LIMA
ALL RECEIVED STAND BY

Once all candidates have responded, the vessel in distress will no longer require assistance. This will be indicated in the usual way with the transmission of seelonce feenee, which should be logged as in entry number 7. In this example the transmission was made at 1110 UTC, but the message to end distress was handled at 1107 UTC. CQ may be used as an abbreviation for 'all stations':

```
MAYDAY
ALL STATIONS ALL STATIONS
ALL STATIONS
THIS IS
MARTHA MARTHA MARTHA
CALLSIGN DELTA HOTEL ALPHA LIMA
MMSI TWO ONE TWO FOUR FOUR FIVE
ZERO EIGHT NINE
TIME ONE ONE ZERO SEVEN UTC
THE VESSEL MARTHA
SEELONCE FEENEE
OUT
```

The last entry, which is number 8 in this example, is to sign yourself off watch. If it were appropriate, you would also put your batteries on charge at this point.

This is just one example of a radiotelephony scenario in order to demonstrate log keeping in detail. The radio regulations only require ships' names and callsigns to be said once with each transmission. However, during the examination, as an aid to log-keeping, ships' names may be spelt and call signs spoken three times. Students may also be required to provide the position information without being prompted to do so by the examiner. However, these transmissions have been included in the example because it provides a more realistic concept of how the communications would happen in practice.

Radio Log Vessel ...SARPEDON............... Callsign ...MGMES.

	Date/Time	To	From	Summary of Communications	Frequency
①	12.09.16 0900 UTC			Position 19°51'N 040°04'W 0900 UTC	
②	1100		212445089	DSC batteries & printer tested D. Brhout. DSC distress alert 20°01'N 040°01'W	2187.5 kHz
③	1101			at 1030 UTC Sinking 33E Set Watch @Brhout	2182 kHz
④	1103	Mayday	DHAL	Mayday Martha DHAL 212445089 in position 20°02'N 040°05'W Sinking require immediate assistance 15 P.O.B. 300m visibility. Over.	
⑤	1106	DHAL	MGMES	R. Mayday Sarpedon	SB "
	1107	DHAL	MPLA6	R. Mayday Argent	SB "
⑥	1108	MGMES	DHAL	Pos? 10 miles bearing 180° from you, speed 20 kn ETA 30 mins.	SB "
	1109	MPLA6	DHAL	Pos? 6 miles bearing 315° from you, speed 8 kn ETA 45 mins.	SB "
⑦	1110	CQ	DHAL	Mayday 1107 UTC Martha Seelonce Feenee. Off watch @Brhout	2182 kHz
⑧					

FIG 19 *Sarpedon's* specimen log

8 The INMARSAT Systems

The ROC course does not cover any of the INMARSAT systems. The LRC course covers the theory of Fleet F77 and SAT C systems but only practical use of SAT C using telex communications. The GOC course covers the theory of Fleet F77 and SAT C systems. It also covers the practical use of Fleet F77 using telephone, as well as SAT C using telex communications.

INMARSAT is a partnership involving over 80 countries. In 1999 it became a Limited Company, owned by all existing signatories. The GMDSS space segment consists of four INMARSAT 3 satellites in geostationary orbit 22,300 miles (35,700 kilometres) above the equator. Backup satellites are also in orbit and could be brought into use if necessary. Geostationary means that they remain stationary relative to a geographical position on earth beneath them. However, the satellites themselves are anything but stationary as they must orbit the earth at a speed in excess of 6,500 miles (10,500 kilometres) an hour in order to maintain their position. The four satellites are each said to have a footprint, which refers to the position on earth from where the satellite is visible and can therefore be used for communications (see Figure 20 on page 82). The limit of each in a north and south direction is 81°, because of the altitude of the satellite and the fact that the earth curves towards the poles. However, since 5° of elevation are required for successful communications, the workable limits are taken to be 76° north and south. There is a large overlap of footprints in an east-west direction, so it is not unusual to have a choice of two or, in some areas, three satellites.

The satellite footprints are referred to as ocean regions. They are: the Pacific Ocean Region (POR), the Indian Ocean Region (IOR), the Atlantic Ocean Region East (AORE) and the Atlantic Ocean Region West (AORW). The Satellite Control Centre (SCC) in London controls and maintains the satellites, ensuring amongst other things that they stay on station. Each terminal on board will have a chart in the software that enables the antenna to find the satellite. If the satellite has drifted off station, the antenna will not be able to find it. Every 4 weeks each satellite will have drifted by about 0.1°. The SCC will make a station-keeping manoeuvre to realign it. This takes about an 11-second burn of the rockets for the east-west adjustment. The north-south adjustment involves the tilt of the satellite and this is carried out every 8 weeks.

Land Earth Stations (LES) perform a similar job to the coast radio stations in terrestrial communications. They provide a link between a vessel, named a Mobile Earth Station (MES), via a satellite to the telephone network and are capable of handling thousands of calls at any one time. Within all ocean regions,

FIG 20 The INMARSAT 3 satellite coverage chart.

both INMARSAT C and Fleet F77 has a single Network Co-ordination Station (NCS) and a network of LESs, some of which will deal with both systems. It is the job of the NCS to monitor traffic and allocate free channels to both the MES and LES in order to facilitate communications. The same four satellites are used for both INMARSAT systems within the GMDSS.

INMARSAT C

INMARSAT C, introduced in 1991, was developed to provide low-cost digital communications. The system requires a lightweight electronic unit (EU), a PC and a small omnidirectional antenna approximately 20 centimetres (8 inches) in diameter. It meets the requirements for GMDSS and supports prepared telex, fax and data transmissions using a store and forward technique. The system uses Time-Division Multiplexing (TDM), meaning that small packets of information are sent from the SAT C terminal when the satellite channel is free. Up to 22 ships can use the same channel simultaneously but in rotation, with the system accepting a packet of information from each ship in turn. This happens automatically with no action being required by the user. The message is reconstituted at the LES and checked for error before it is sent on to its destination, hence the term 'store and forward'. The technique puts a delay of several minutes into the system, so neither voice communications nor live telex are possible. SAT C is particularly useful for receiving Enhanced Group Calling (EGC) services. SafetyNET, used to broadcast MSI, the satellite equivalent to Navtex, is one such service and is free of charge. FleetNET is a subscription service that is used to send confidential information to individual vessels or groups of vessels – for example, race participants could receive specialist weather information. In the future the functionality of SAT C will be enhanced.

INMARSAT FLEET F77

Fleet F77, introduced in 2005, brings a new dimension to INMARSAT's portfolio and will continue within GMDSS until 2021. It features prioritisation and pre-emption, ensuring non-essential communications will be terminated, so that more urgent traffic can be sent. Distress will pre-empt all other communications. Urgency will pre-empt everything other than distress, and so on.

Fleet F77 also offers two data services for internet and e-mail: Mobile Packet Data Service (MPDS) and mobile Integrated Services Digital Network (ISDN).

The mobile ISDN uses a dedicated channel between your terminal and the LES. You are charged for the total time this channel is allocated to you. It supports Internet Protocol and File Transfer Protocol and is best used for large files and video conferencing or when speed is important.

MPDS sends your data in packets over the network. You can share the channel with other users, in a similar way to Sat C, as MPDS allows for simultaneous connections. At times when you may be typing an e-mail or reading a web page, the channel is free for others to use. You are not charged for the time you are connected, but for amount of data you send and receive, so you can always stay online.

ISDN and MPDS data sessions are regarded as routine and so will be terminated if a higher priority telephone call is initiated. If a routine telephone call is received during a data session and the call is accepted, the data session will be terminated. If the call is rejected the data session will be allowed to continue.

OPERATIONS

Before communications can commence, the associated antenna must have an unobstructed view of a satellite. Fleet F77 use a large steerable antenna producing a pencil beam that must point at one of the satellites. On most systems this can be achieved automatically. Once a signal has been detected, the antenna will lock on to it and track the satellite, unless the ship's heading puts it into a blind arc. For example,

Antenna for INMARSAT C.

if an alteration of course puts the antenna behind a funnel, the line of sight to the satellite will be lost, which is something to bear in mind during distress communications. To find the satellite manually, the operator must know its azimuth and elevation. The azimuth is the bearing to the satellite, through 360° around the horizon. The elevation is the angle of the satellite, up to 90° above the horizon. Tables and charts are published to enable operators to calculate the satellite's azimuth and elevation from a given position on earth. The antenna is driven by servo motors.

In practice there may be a choice of satellites, each offering a range of LESs with differing services. Updated information on services can be obtained through SAT C and from INMARSAT themselves. Heavy users of the system can often negotiate discounted rates and service providers sometimes offer incentives to use them. It is, therefore, worth investigating the options before making a choice. To contact a ship from on shore, the maritime access code +870 is the equivalent to the terrestrial country codes. The original INMARSAT Ocean Region codes were discontinued on 31 December 2008. +870 followed by the vessel's INMARSAT identification number will now reach any INMARSAT terminal anywhere in the world.

SAT C operates slightly differently, using a small omni-directional antenna that is functional virtually up to the edge of the satellite footprint. With this system the vessel must log in to a satellite. The satellite continually transmits on the common signalling channel, with which the equipment will synchronise during the log-in procedure. Once this is done, the NCS in control of SAT C services through the chosen satellite will automatically route any messages to the vessel. To ensure that messages are not lost and the NCS time is not wasted, it is important to log out before switching the SAT C terminal off. More details will be found in Chapter 9. With some terminals it is possible to log in by scanning for the strongest signal. This is not the best option as the NCS could change as the signal strength varies and SafetyNET messages could be lost. More importantly, you do not want the NCS to change in the middle of distress working, as discussed in Chapter 9. It is always best to tune to a specific NCS and make that the preferred ocean region. Your choice may be influenced by the SafetyNET broadcasts you wish to receive – for example, the AORE satellite transmits Navarea 1 information (see Chapter 12 for more details).

TWO-DIGIT SPECIAL SERVICE CODES

Once connected to an LES, in routine priority, many of them offer several Short Access Code (SAC) services. The special service two-digit code will be followed by # (hash) if using the telephone. For example, code 32 is available with both systems and will connect to someone who can give medical advice. Code 38 is used for medical assistance or medical evacuation and 39 for maritime assistance, again available through both systems. The system will route you to a doctor or MRCC in the same country as the LES that you selected. Calls using codes 32, 38 and 39 are free of charge and are only to be used for urgency communications.

Safety code 41 is used to report meteorological observations and 42 to report a navigational hazard. Code 43 is used to report a ship's position to AMVER, which is a global voluntary reporting system that is open to any flag state.

Choosing urgent or safety priority will initiate priorisation and pre-emption on Fleet F77. However, the connection can still be made if the terminal is left in routine priority, and a free telephone line is available.

To help you remember

Urgency	Safety
32 WHAT DO WE DO?	**41** WHERE IS THE SUN?
38 EVACUATE	**42** I WILL SINK YOU!
39 MARITIME	**43** WHERE ARE WE?

DISTRESS PRIORITY CONNECTION FLEET F77

A distress priority connection ensures instant routing to an MRCC. The process is totally automatic and does not involve a human operator. Operators are made aware of the fact that a distress priority call has passed through their station by the use of alarms. The LES will then provide an automatic priority connection to its local MRCC. The NCS in each region will monitor the progress of such a call and will intervene if any problems are detected. If the call has been addressed to an LES that cannot be worked through the chosen satellite, the NCS will accept the call on its behalf. Any call sent with distress priority is therefore almost certain to succeed. The Fleet F77 software is capable of selecting an LES on behalf of the operator, using a pre-programmed default system.

DISTRESS ALERTING ON SAT C

Sat C equipment designed after 1997 will not allow alerts to be sent via the keyboard alone but will require the lifting of a cover to enable the activation of one or two dedicated distress buttons. Operators using SAT C terminals can choose an LES and associated MRCC.

AVOIDING FALSE ALERTS

Do not allow distress priority to be selected unless the vessel has a distress situation to report. If the terminal has any complicated functions, make sure that they are displayed next to the unit for all to see. Ensure that all personnel who use the equipment are either thoroughly trained or closely supervised. The manufacturer's instructions should always be studied carefully before any equipment is used.

CANCELLING FALSE ALERTS

If a false distress alert is sent from a Sat C terminal, it is important to notify the MRCC using a distress priority message via the same satellite and LES. The message should include the ship's name, callsign, INMARSAT C identification number, the fact that the alert should be cancelled as it was sent in error, and the time in UTC that it was sent. It is imperative that any operator who knowingly sends a false alert does not ignore the situation.

SECURITY

In order to prevent the corruption of software used for distress, urgency or safety communications, a dedicated computer is recommended.

Questions

1 Name the INMARSAT ocean regions.

2 Which system uses a store and forward technique?

3 Which system uses a small omnidirectional antenna?

4 What is meant by a satellite's footprint?

5 Why is it important to log out before switching off a SAT C terminal?

6 Which two-digit code would you use to obtain medical advice over the telephone?

7 What should you do if you send a distress alert in error on INMARSAT C?

8 Who is responsible for allocating channels for telephone calls?

Answers

1 There are four INMARSAT ocean regions. They are the Pacific Ocean Region (POR), the Indian Ocean Region (IOR), the Atlantic Ocean Region East (AORE) and the Atlantic Ocean Region West (AORW).

2 SAT C uses a store and forward technique.

3 SAT C uses a small omnidirectional antenna.

4 Each satellite is said to have a footprint, which refers to the position on earth from where the satellite is visible and can therefore be used for communications.

5 It is important to log out before switching the SAT C terminal off to ensure that messages are not lost and the NCS time is not wasted.

6 To obtain medical advice over the telephone, 32# would be used. Selecting urgent priority will initiate prioritisation and pre-emption.

7 If a distress alert is sent in error, it is important to notify the MRCC using a distress priority message via the same satellite and LES. The message should include the ship's name, callsign, INMARSAT identification number, the fact that the alert should be cancelled, and the time in UTC that it was sent.

8 The NCS is responsible for allocating channels for telephone calls.

9 INMARSAT Procedures

Geostationary satellites have to be at a high altitude in order to provide a large workable footprint. The fact that the signal has to travel in excess of 45,000 miles (72,000 kilometres) between a Mobile Earth Station (MES) and a Land Earth Station (LES) introduces approximately one-quarter of a second time delay into communications. Remember that in times of distress this system will not alert nearby vessels to your situation because it is a point-to-point system. This is similar to dialling 999 from home, where your neighbour does not know that you are in trouble and cannot help you.

INMARSAT FLEET F77 TELEPHONE

Priority connections

Calling using Fleet F77 is achieved by a priority connection through one of the satellites. The priorities are distress, urgency, safety and routine, or P3, P2, P1 or P0 on older equipment. During the set-up procedure a default LES in each ocean region must be nominated for receipt of distress calls.

Distress priority connection

- LIFT THE TELEPHONE HANDSET
- PRESS AND HOLD THE DISTRESS PUSH-BUTTON FOR SIX SECONDS
- PRESS # TO INITIATE THE CALL

If the connection is not successful within 15 seconds, the procedure should be repeated. This is a similar concept to picking up the telephone at home. If you dialled a number and nothing happened within 15 seconds, you would hang up and try again.

Once the connection has been made (the equivalent of the call in radio-telephony procedures) the message should be spoken.

Distress message

M MAYDAY

I IDENTIFICATION – NAME, CALLSIGN AND FLEET F77 NUMBER

P POSITION

N NATURE OF THE DISTRESS

A ASSISTANCE REQUIRED

N NUMBER ON BOARD

O OTHER INFORMATION

O OVER

DISTRESS RELAY CONNECTION

There is no facility for a distress relay connection, therefore a distress priority connection should be made. However, it is imperative to commence the message with Mayday Relay. This will make it clear to the MRCC at the start that you are not the vessel in distress.

Urgency priority connection

- LIFT THE HANDSET
- SELECT THE APPROPRIATE LES IDENTIFICATION CODE
- INPUT THE TWO DIGIT CODE
- SELECT URGENT PRIORITY (if prioritisation and pre-emption is required)
- PRESS # TO INITIATE THE CALL

The relevant two-digit code should be used: 32 for medical advice, 38 for medical assistance or medical evacuation and 39 for maritime assistance.

Urgency message

P PAN PAN

I IDENTIFICATION – NAME, CALLSIGN AND FLEET F77 NUMBER

P POSITION

N NATURE OF THE URGENCY

A ASSISTANCE REQUIRED

N NUMBER ON BOARD (if relevant)

O OTHER INFORMATION

O OVER

Fleet F77 distress button and
telephone handset.

Safety priority connection

- LIFT THE HANDSET
- SELECT THE APPROPRIATE LES IDENTIFICATION CODE
- INPUT THE TWO DIGIT CODE
- SELECT SAFETY PRIORITY (if prioritisation and pre-emption is required)
- PRESS # TO INITIATE THE CALL

The relevant two-digit code should be used: 41 to report a meteorological observation, 42 to report a navigational hazard or 43 to report your ship's position to AMVER.

Safety message

S SÉCURITÉ

I IDENTIFICATION – NAME, CALLSIGN AND FLEET F77 NUMBER

NAVIGATION WARNING AT 2000 UTC

P POSITION

N NATURE OF THE SAFETY MESSAGE

A ADVICE

O OUT

Routine priority connection

- LIFT THE HANDSET
- SELECT THE APPROPRIATE LES IDENTIFICATION CODE
- Routine priority should be the default option
- INPUT 00 for automatic dialling
  COUNTRY CODE or MARITIME ACCESS CODE 870 if calling another vessel
  SUBSCRIBER'S TELEPHONE NUMBER or INMARSAT NUMBER
- PRESS # TO INITIATE THE CALL

As always, the manufacturer's instruction manual should be studied with care before the terminal is used.

INMARSAT C

Distress alerting

There are two ways of alerting by SAT C:

- UNDESIGNATED – PRESS ONE OR TWO DISTRESS BUTTONS (typically for three or five seconds)

OR

- DESIGNATED – SELECT DISTRESS ALERT FROM THE MENU, INPUT THE DESIGNATION AND REQUIRED LES CODE, THEN PRESS ONE OR TWO DISTRESS BUTTONS (typically for three or five seconds)

If no acknowledgement is received within five minutes following either method, repeat the alert. Remember that this is a store and forward system, which accounts for the longer response time. Distress alerts can be sent before the terminal is logged in, and before the equipment is commissioned, so care should always be taken not to send distress alerts in error.

The distress alert sent by pressing the button(s) on the electronic unit will be an undesignated alert giving the ship's identification and last entered position.

If the menu is accessed, more information can be given. Choosing from a list of distress situations can designate the alert. The vessel's position can be updated if this has not been done automatically by GPS. The course and speed can be included in the alert with information taken from the GPS input. Any LES in the ocean region can be chosen and then the button(s) should be pressed to transmit the alert, which will be routed via the LES to its associated MRCC. This is the best option, because the LES is selected.

It is important at this stage to ensure that the automatic scan facility is set to scan only the ocean region to which the terminal was logged in when the alert

INMARSAT C distress buttons.

was sent. This is achieved by making it the preferred ocean region. If another region is indicated as the preferred one and signal strength increases on the common signalling channel from the NCS of that ocean region, the equipment will retune and communications with the MRCC will be lost.

Whilst the operator is waiting for a response, the distress message should be prepared along the same lines as before with the standard MIPNANOO. The terminal must be logged in to an NCS to send the message.

Distress message

Start with a blank line.

M MAYDAY

I IDENTIFICATION – NAME, CALLSIGN AND SAT C NUMBER

P POSITION

N NATURE OF THE DISTRESS

A ASSISTANCE REQUIRED

N NUMBER ON BOARD

O OTHER INFORMATION

O OVER (or NNNN because this is sent in store and forward mode)

To transmit the distress message be sure to choose distress priority. This will ensure that you are allocated a distress priority channel through the satellite. It is important to use the same LES that was used for the alert, so that the message is received by the same MRCC. If an undesignated alert was sent, you may have to wait for the acknowledgement to discover which LES was allocated to you, before you can send the message.

Other priority messages

SAT C transmission priorities are either routine or distress.

Distress relay messages are sent in distress priority and commence 'Mayday Relay', making it clear to the MRCC that you are not in distress. A distress alert would not precede this message.

Urgency and safety messages have to be sent from the terminal under routine priority. With this system, the special service two-digit codes will ensure the required priority connection from the LES.

To send a prepared routine message, select routine priority. The country code, fax number, or telex number and answerback of the destination subscriber are required. If this is a subscriber you contact frequently, the details may be chosen from your destination directory. Select the LES and initiate the call. The message will then be transferred to the electronic unit and sent.

Performance Verification Test

This is sometimes called a link test. It does limit system functionality whilst in progress and is time consuming. Once running it will test the link to the LES and report signal quality, then transmit and receive a test message. The ability to send a distress alert is also tested.

Logging out

It is important to log out before switching off the INMARSAT C terminal. Logging out informs the NCS of the ocean region that the terminal is no longer available to accept messages and callers will be informed of this fact. If the operator does not log out, the LES will continue to try to send messages to the vessel and eventually the messages could be lost. Repeated attempts could also prove to be expensive to the subscriber who is trying to call.

Questions

1 You are in position 31° 24´ S 051° 31´ W, your vessel's name is Jade, callsign MENO4, INMARSAT Fleet F77 mobile number 764095687. You have complete engine failure and need to call for maritime assistance by telephone. State the procedure that you should follow and the voice message that you should send.

2 You are in position 01° 13´ S 002° 11´ E, your course is 090° at a speed of 5 knots. Your vessel's name is Jupiter, callsign GPLO5, INMARSAT Fleet F77 number 763356789,. There are 40 persons on board. You have discovered a fire and need to call for immediate assistance. Two of the crew have been badly burned. State the procedure that you should follow and the message that you should send.

3 You are in position 29° 53´ N 031° 32´ W. Your vessel's name is Saturn, callsign MRAX9, INMARSAT C mobile number 423334567. You have struck a submerged object and are sinking. There are 25 persons on board and the sea state is rough. State the procedure that you should follow and the message that you should send.

Answers

1 Lift the handset

Select the LES identification code

Enter 39 for maritime assistance

Select urgent priority

Press # to initiate the call.

Once connected, speak:

Pan Pan
Jade MENO4 764095687
In position 31° 24´ S 051° 31´ W
Complete engine failure
Require maritime assistance
Over

2 Lift the handset

Press and hold the distress push-button for six seconds

Wait for an automatic connection to an MRCC

Mayday
Jupiter GPLO5 763356789
In position 01° 13´ S 002° 11´ E
Course 090° speed 5 knots
Fire on board
Require immediate assistance
40 persons on board, two need urgent medical attention
Over

3 Either press and hold the distress button(s) on the electronic unit, or preferably select distress alert from the menu, select designation and LES code and then press and hold the distress button(s). Next type and send the following message, with distress priority, via the same LES, starting with a blank line:

Mayday

Saturn MRAX9, 423334567

In position 29° 53´ N 031° 32´ W

Sinking

Require immediate assistance

25 persons on board

Sea conditions are rough

Over (or NNNN)

Check that the ocean region that you have used is selected as your preferred ocean region, to prevent change of NCS during distress working.

10 EPIRBs and SARTs

Emergency Position Indicating Radio Beacons (EPIRBs) and Search And Rescue Transponders (SARTs) provide locating and homing signals for use during Search And Rescue (SAR) operations. The EPIRB usually provides a 'ball park' position for the search, with the SART providing the 'fine tune' facility for location of the survivors. If at all possible, keep both with you if you need to abandon your ship.

EPIRBs

GMDSS regulations require the vessel to carry at least two independent means of transmitting a distress alert. The EPIRB provides a secondary method of distress alerting. It relays position and identification information from a casualty in distress to an MRCC. The EPIRB signal indicates that one or more persons are in distress, that they may no longer be on board their vessel and that they may not have receiving facilities.

COSPAS/SARSAT EPIRBs

COSPAS/SARSAT is an international humanitarian Search And Rescue (SAR) system. EPIRBs are for use in all sea areas and communicate with designated satellites between 406.025 and 406.037 MHz (usually referred to as 406 MHz). 121.5 MHz has not been detected by the satellites since 1st February 2009 but is still often included in the EPIRB as a homing signal. There are more than one million beacons in use worldwide.

Low Altitude Earth Orbit (LEO)

The original Low altitude Earth Orbit (LEO) space segment is operated jointly by the Russian Federation and an American-Canadian-French consortium. The Russian payload is COSPAS – COsmicheskaya Sistyema Poiska Avariynich Sudov, which translates as Space System for the Search of Vessels in Distress. The American-Canadian-French payload is SARSAT – Search And Rescue Satellite Aided Tracking. There are many other participating nations in the programme that provide electronics and ground support.

COSPAS started as an electronic package on the Russian NADEZHDA navigation satellites. However, these navigation systems are now supported by GLONASS. There have therefore been no operational COSPAS payloads on LEO satellites since September 2007.

SARSAT is currently an instrument package on a number of the NOAA weather satellites and the EUMETSAT MetOp-A satellite has been carrying a payload since October 2006.

COSPAS/SARSAT came on line in 1982 and is comprised of a number of LEO satellites in displaced, near-polar orbits that are able to scan the entire globe every 2–3 hours. The orbits are set and the earth rotates beneath them. The system is designed to have at least four satellites in operation at all times, although there are often more. The low altitude of these satellites means that the transmitter power of the 406 MHz EPIRB need only be 5 watts. The altitude is typically 530 miles (850 kilometres) and travelling at 4 miles (7 kilometres) per second they can orbit the earth every 100 minutes. The circular footprint is approximately 3,730 miles (6,000 kilometres) in diameter and the satellite crosses the sky in about 15 minutes.

Once an EPIRB is activated the beacon transmits a digitally encoded distress alert, which includes the identification of the ship, often in the form of a 15 hexa-decimal code. Each satellite carries an SAR processor, which receives on 406 MHz and stores any distress alerts from beacons that it passes over. The alert will then be retransmitted either immediately if a ground station is in view, or as soon as one comes into the footprint.

The satellites communicate worldwide with a large network of ground stations on earth, called Local User Terminals (LUTs), which track the satellites using parabolic antennae. The average notification time is 45 minutes, because there is not continual coverage by the satellites. There may be a time delay before the next satellite passes over the beacon and then another delay for it to be in a suitable position to relay the information to a LEOLUT. One pass is usually sufficient for the 406 MHz beacon with a stable signal, although if reception is poor it may require a second pass.

The LEOLUT uses Doppler frequency analysis to calculate the position of the EPIRB, using the motion of the satellite relative to the stationary beacon on the earth's surface. The location accuracy is said to be within 3 miles (5 kilometres). However, most location calculations are significantly more accurate than this.

The position is then routed to a Mission Control Centre (MCC) via a network connection. The MCC will decode the identification information contained within the transmission. All of the information is then passed on to an MRCC.

Final location is achieved by a low power 121.5 MHz homing signal that is included in most 406 MHz beacons. 121.5 MHz is the international aeronautical emergency frequency and whilst not mandatory, the SAR aircraft find it useful for homing. It is also possible that a passing aircraft will pick up the signal.

It is very important to ensure that any EPIRB is correctly programmed and registered.

Geostationary Earth Orbit (GEO)

Research into the use of geostationary satellites for receiving signals from 406 MHz GPS-encoding beacons started in 1987. The system has been named the Geostationary Earth Orbit Search And Rescue (GEOSAR) system. The GEO satellites are at an altitude of 22,370 miles (36,000 kilometres) and communicate with GEOLUTs. This generation of beacons maintain all the LEO functions but have the addition of a GPS. They are widely available and much more efficient.

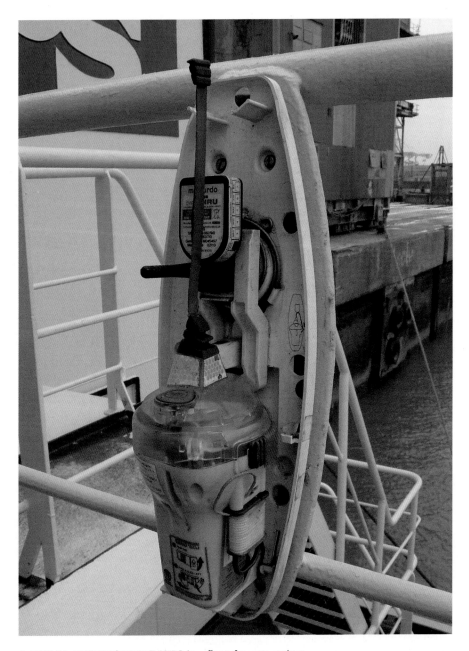

A 406 MHz COSPAS/SARSAT EPIRB in a float-free mounting.

Notification time is reduced to a few minutes and positioning is as accurate as GPS. If the GPS fails or if the vessel trades above 70°, then the original 406 MHz part of the beacon will continue to work. The option to include an AIS transmitter in these beacons became available in 2016.

Medium Altitude Earth Orbit (MEO) – the Future

In 2011 the Russian Federation's GLONASS-K No1 was launched, hosting the first Medium altitude Earth Orbit Search And Rescue (MEOSAR) payload, in an orbit 13,670 miles (22,000 kilometres) above the earth. This joined experimental Distress Alerting Satellite System (DASS) payloads on the USA's GPS satellites. MEOSAR payloads have also been included on the new European GALILEO navigation satellites.

The MEOSAR satellites are predicted to grow to large numbers over the next few years with a network of MEOLUTs to receive transmissions from GPS and GLONASS, with possibly a separate ground segment for GALILEO.

Once sufficient MEOSAR satellite payloads and receiving ground stations are available worldwide, the system will be declared operational.

Due to the fact that there will now be so many satellites available, several should simultaneously receive and relay any distress alert to several different ground stations, thus increasing the probability of detection. Position will be calculated by triangulation, based on the time the signal is received, rather than the Doppler calculations required for LEO or the transmitting of a GPS position for GEO systems. The result will be that MEOSAR beacons should be much less expensive to produce. It is expected that the new beacons will have the ability to include additional information in the alert and have a return-link, which will allow acknowledgements to be sent back to the beacon.

MEOSAR will supplement the current system, have full operational compatibility with it, give near instantaneous global coverage and provide highly accurate location information. The objective is to locate within 100 metres 95% of the time, in less than five minutes, even for beacons not equipped with GPS.

ACTIVATION

EPIRBs can be either manually or automatically activated. If the automatic system is chosen, a hydrostatic release is fitted, which will allow the EPIRB to float free when immersed to a depth of approximately 4 metres. Regulations require all compulsorily fitted vessels to install a float-free EPIRB. To help reduce the false alarm rate, most new EPIRBs are being produced with a two-stage activation process. The first action will arm it, for example by removing it from its housing. The second action will activate it, for example by manually switching it on or immersing it in sea water.

SARTs

The purpose of a Search And Rescue Transponder (SART) is to indicate the position of persons or vessels in distress. It operates on 9 GHz, also known as the X band or the three centimetre radar band. A transponder is a unit that transmits in response to an incoming signal. A SART will transmit its signals when interrogated by a radar producing a pulse with a wavelength of three centimetres. The transmission is line of sight, so range is unlikely to be more than 10 miles to a ship but it will be much greater, maybe 30 to 40 miles, to a search and rescue aircraft (see Figure 21). Rough conditions will produce a greater range on the crests of

FIG 21 The range of a SART transmission is line of sight, typically five nautical miles to a ship with an antenna height of 15 metres and up to 40 nautical miles to an aircraft searching at 3,000 feet.

waves but loss of signal in the troughs. Flat calm conditions are not ideal as radar pulses can be reflected from the surface of the sea. The SART will sound an alarm and change its light characteristic when interrogated by a vessel close at hand, which is sure to raise morale. When this happens, call on VHF channel 16 and fire flares. The battery should allow for 96 hours in stand-by mode followed by eight hours of transmitting time. Do not deploy a SART and a radar reflector simultaneously as the reflector may obscure the SART. If the SART is interrogated, it sweeps through the radar frequency band 12 times. When the SART frequency matches that of the interrogating radar during each sweep, it will produce a target on the radar screen.

Twelve dots approximately 0.64 of a nautical mile apart will be shown on the screen (see Figure 22). The dot closest to the ship's position indicates the position of the SART. When the range to the SART closes to under one mile, the dots will change into arcs (see Figure 23). At this point, the position of the casualty is accurate to within 150 metres. As the range closes even further, concentric circles will be seen (see Figure 24). When searching for a SART, choose a radar range between 6 and 12 nautical miles because the 12 dots may extend to nearly 10 miles beyond the position of the SART. If the radar is on a short range and only one or two dots are displayed, they could be confused with other targets.

FIG 22 Twelve dots will be shown on the radar screen of a search vessel.

FIG 23 When the range closes to under one mile, the dots change into arcs.

FIG 24 As the range closes further, the arcs change into concentric circles.

A SART should be positioned upright and as high as possible. It should be at least one metre above sea level.

AIS-SART

From the 1st January 2010, the Automatic Identification System – Search And Rescue Transmitter (AIS-SART) joined the GMDSS, as an alternative to the radar SART.

The AIS-SART is programmed with a nine-digit identification code. The first three digits being 970, the following two digits are a manufacturer code and the last four a serial number. This is not a unique ID and cannot identify the vessel. It has an internal GPS to enable it to receive position information and battery life is 96 hours.

Once activated, the AIS-SART transmits eight messages, over a 14-second time slot, every minute, on two different VHF channels. One channel operates on 161.975 MHz, the other on 162.025 MHz, and four messages will be sent on each. It is only necessary to receive one of these messages to obtain an accurate location. However, sending multiple messages ensures that this will happen.

Any equipment capable of receiving an AIS signal can also detect an AIS-SART. The identification appears, along with the time, position, range and bearing. It is also displayed on electronic charts as a cross enclosed by a small circle.

The range is line of sight, so comparable to the radar SART. However, there is no AIS receiver, so unlike the radar SART it is unable to inform you that your signal has been received by nearby vessels.

AIS-SART	
ID:	970221234
UTC:	16 : 15 : 30
LAT:	50° 14.450' N
LON:	010° 18.034' W
RANGE:	3.48 nm 184°

TESTING OF EPIRBs AND SARTs

EPIRBs and SARTs must be tested monthly in accordance with the manufacturer's instructions. Take care, as the SART is tested with a live transmission. At this time, also inspect the units for signs of damage or corrosion. Check lanyards, seals, telescopic poles and battery expiry dates of the SARTs. EPIRBs, lanyards and sea water contacts should be checked and if it is intended that the unit should float free, ensure that it could do so in an emergency. The batteries and hydrostatic release should be changed if the expiry date is close. Some units will need to be returned to the manufacturer at this time. It has been reported that some 406 MHz EPIRBs pass their internal test but do not transmit if required to do so. It is advisable to have EPIRBs tested annually with a shielded tester that will receive and decode the 406 MHz signal, check the identification and, if appropriate, provide an audible indication that the 121.5 MHz homing signal is functioning.

AIS-SART.

AVOIDING FALSE ALERTS

During each safety drill, instruction should be given in the use of EPIRBs and SARTs.

It is important to ensure that EPIRBs are properly registered and that registrations are updated if the unit changes hands. Failure to do so can result in heavy penalties. Falmouth Coastguard administers the UK EPIRB register. The EPIRB should not be activated if assistance has been made available by other means. If possible, an EPIRB should be retrieved and deactivated after use. If it is to be scrapped, it should be made inoperable. If it is to be returned for maintenance, it should be either disabled or wrapped in two layers of aluminium foil. Every effort should be made to ensure that the EPIRB does not transmit accidentally. Should this happen, it must be switched off immediately and a coast station or MRCC informed.

Questions

1 What is the purpose of an EPIRB?

2 What does the EPIRB signal indicate?

3 What is the primary frequency used by a COSPAS/SARSAT EPIRB and in which sea areas may it be used?

4 Which frequency is used for the low power homing signal of an EPIRB?

5 What is the purpose of a radar SART?

6 On which frequency does a radar SART operate?

7 To which signal does the radar SART respond?

8 How would you recognise a radar SART transmission on a radar screen?

9 How would you know that you were closing on the casualty?

10 Where is an AIS SART signal displayed?

11 How would you recognise an AIS SART transmission?

12 How often should the SART and EPIRB be tested?

13 What is involved in testing the EPIRB and the SART?

14 What should you do if your EPIRB is activated in error?

Answers

1 The purpose of an EPIRB is to provide a secondary means of distress alerting as well as identification and position information regarding the casualty.

2 The EPIRB signal indicates that one or more persons are in distress, that they may no longer be on board their vessel and that they may not have receiving facilities.

3 The frequency used by a COSPAS/SARSAT EPIRB is 406 MHz and it may be used in areas A1, A2, A3 and A4.

4 121.5 MHz is used for the low power homing signal of an EPIRB.

5 The purpose of a radar SART is to indicate the position of persons or vessels in distress by means of a three centimetre radar.

6 A radar SART operates on 9 GHz, also known as the X band.

7 The radar SART responds to a signal from a three centimetre radar.

8 A radar SART transmission appears on a radar screen as 12 dots. The dot closest to the ship's position is the SART.

9 When you close to under one mile, the dots start to arc and eventually form concentric circles as the SART's position is approached.

10 An AIS SART signal is displayed on any equipment capable of receiving an AIS signal.

11 An AIS SART is displayed as a nine digit number commencing 970, and a cross within a circle on electronic charts.

12 The SART and EPIRB must be tested monthly.

13 Carry out the tests in accordance with the manufacturer's instructions. At the same time, inspect the units for signs of damage or corrosion. Check lanyards, seals, telescopic poles and battery expiry dates of the SARTs. EPIRBs, lanyards and sea water contacts should be checked and if it is intended that the unit should float free, ensure that it could do so in an emergency. The batteries and hydrostatic release should be changed if the expiry date is close.

14 If your EPIRB is activated in error, it should be switched off immediately and a coast station or MRCC notified.

11 Antennae and Batteries

Picture a stone being thrown into a pond on a very still day. Ripples will move out from the position where the stone entered the water. Each wave will increase in diameter and weaken as it moves away from the source. If a duck was sitting on the pond, it would move up and down on each wave as it passed. This is how two antennae react to each other. The transmitting antenna produces oscillating electromagnetic energy at, for example, 150 watts, which travels through free space, becoming weaker with distance. A receiving antenna will receive the energy in perhaps microwatts, which it will then amplify to an appropriate level to be heard at the loud speaker.

VHF ANTENNA

The VHF transceiver is connected to either a dipole or a whip antenna, which can be full, half or quarter the wavelength of channel 16 which is 156.8 MHz.

The full whip antenna is a little less than two metres long, insulated at the bottom and made of wire encapsulated in glassfibre. VHF antennae should be situated as high as possible since the range of VHF communications is determined by the height of the antennae. Since the radio wave is polarised along the axis of the antennae, it is not recommended that it be raked back in 'go faster' fashion. In this orientation, a large proportion of the radiated power will be horizontally polarised and therefore not received by vertical receiving antennae. When using transportable radios try to hold them upright for the same reason. This puts the antenna fairly close to the user's eye. It is therefore not recommended to use a transportable that transmits at more than six watts in order to minimise the health risk.

Above: Whip antennae and radomes.

An antenna tuning unit (ATU).

MF AND HF WHIP ANTENNA

A whip antenna may be used for MF and HF communications. It will vary in length depending on the size of the vessel and type of installation. However, it is often between 7.5 and 9 metres (25 and 30 feet) long and constructed of metal sections encased in glassfibre, which screw together and lock in place. A wire aerial is not aesthetically pleasing. The whip antenna is therefore a popular alternative and is used on most modern ships. For the antenna to function efficiently, its length must proportionally match the wavelength of the frequency to be used by the transmitter. An antenna tuning unit (ATU), containing capacitors, adjustable coils and a central processing unit, is used to tune the whip over a variable frequency range. This is activated either by a tune button on the transceiver, or automatically when the PTT is pressed. For optimum performance, the ATU should be situated directly beneath the antenna and ideally above decks.

WIRE AERIAL

Wire aerials are less popular, but do provide excellent radiation properties on MF. They are usually constructed of strong stranded bronze or copper wire with a ceramic or glass insulator at each end. The insulators prevent the wire halyards from forming part of the aerial. If the radio installation is amidships, a T installation is used and if the installation is aft, an inverted L installation is used. Halyards, which control the aerial, should be made from metal, making them fire proof. Another important part of the construction is the weak link (see Figure 26). This has approximately half the breaking strength of the aerial and provides a controlled breaking point if the aerial comes under too much strain. The weak link is always protected by a safety loop to ensure that the aerial does not fall to the deck and also to maintain its usability.

FIG 25 A weak link is used to protect a wire aerial.

When the backstay aerial is used on a yacht, it is under a lot of strain and glass insulators are not strong enough. Special non-conducting carbon fibre insulators are used instead.

Antennae used for MF, HF and VHF communications are omnidirectional.

ANTENNAE FOR INMARSAT FLEET F77

This system requires a large parabolic steerable antenna, which produces a pencil beam. The beam must be aimed to within 5° of the satellite's position. The satellite itself must be at least 5° above the horizon in order to effect reliable communications. Once in auto-tracking mode, the antenna will track the satellite in any sea conditions as long as the ship's heading does not put it into a blind arc. In order to function correctly at all times, the gyro stabilised antenna must have a 360° view of the horizon. Placing of the antenna therefore requires careful consideration. These systems consume large amounts of power and need good control measures to keep them functioning correctly. It should be remembered that in times of distress, when available power may be reduced, the system will only function if the pencil beam is pointing at a satellite, therefore emergency power supplies must be in place.

Fleet F77 supports speech, so a wide bandwidth is needed and the 50 to 100 watt transmitter output is therefore spread fairly thinly. A dish or parabolic reflector is a means of focusing or concentrating the signal from an omni-directional antenna into a narrow pencil beam. An example of an omnidirectional light is a bare light bulb hanging from a light fitting. If the same bulb was fitted into a large torch with a reflector, the resulting beam would be focused, stronger and brighter. The same is true of the resulting radio wave reaching the satellite – it appears to have come from a much more powerful transmitting source. The bigger the dish, the narrower the resulting beam and the stronger the signal.

Fleet F77 antennae are approximately 84 centimetres (33 inches) in diameter, 88 centimetres (35 inches) high and weigh approximately 27 kilograms (60 pounds). Size and weight will vary from one design to another.

ANTENNAE FOR INMARSAT C

This system does not support voice. It therefore uses a narrow bandwidth. The transmitter power output is 50 watts, which gives a strong signal with this bandwidth, so a small omnidirectional antenna can be used. The antenna can be approximately 22 centimetres (8.5 inches) in diameter, 32 centimetres (12.5 inches) high and weigh approximately seven kilograms (15.5 pounds). Some makes are as small as 15 x 13 centimetres (6 x 5 inches) and weigh less than one kilogram (2.2 pounds).

MAINTENANCE OF ANTENNAE

The Fleet F77 satellite communication antenna is covered and protected by a radome. This needs to be kept clean in order to allow radio waves to pass through. Warm soapy water should be used to remove any salt deposits, dirt or soot. It is important not to stand in front of the radome when it is being used, as there is a danger to health. It is therefore imperative to turn off the respective terminal during cleaning to ensure that it is not used. Special paints can now be used on radomes that allow the passage of radio waves.

All terrestrial communication antennae have insulators, which should be kept clean by washing regularly with warm soapy water. They should never be painted. Inspect the insulators for signs of burns or damage, and check all connections, earthing plates and straps.

It is very important that the communications equipment is not used to transmit when maintenance is being carried out, as resulting radiation burns can be horrific. Switch the antenna to ground, if you have this facility, to discharge static.

BATTERIES

Lead acid batteries consist of lead plates surrounded by sulphuric acid mixed with distilled water. On discharge, the chemical reaction between the plates and the electrolyte produces electricity. Great care must always be taken with them, to protect both yourself and your vessel from acid burns and explosion. Hydrogen gas, which is explosive, is produced during charging. If charging continues once the battery is fully charged, the acid will heat up and severe gassing will occur. Many chargers will detect when the battery is fully charged and switch off or reduce to trickle charging, which is often one-tenth of the normal rate. In view of the dangers of hydrogen gas, no machinery in the battery compartment should be capable of producing a spark and the area should be well ventilated at all times.

Marine installations are typically either 12 or 24 volts. The capacity of a battery is usually measured in ampere hours. For example, a one ampere hour battery could produce one amp for one hour, or half an amp for two hours, etc. When batteries are connected in parallel, the total ampere hours is the sum of all the individual batteries' ampere hours.

Rechargeable batteries will always provide better service if they are allowed to fully discharge before fully recharging. Spare batteries are advisable in order to have fully charged batteries available at all times, as required by the radio regulations. Batteries should not be left discharged for long periods of time because there is then a danger that they will fail to recharge.

BATTERY MAINTENANCE

Battery voltage should be tested daily with the battery on load and the charger switched off. First measure the off load voltage. When the battery is put on load, you should not see a drop of more than 10%. Weekly tests should be carried out on reserve sources of energy, for example a motor generator. Monthly tests should involve a thorough inspection of the battery compartment to check the condition of the installation. Always wear goggles and protective clothing when working with batteries. Terminals should be checked for deposits, cleaned and greased. Remove the covers and ensure that the electrolyte is covering the plates. If not, top up with distilled water.

During charging and discharging the specific gravity (relative density) of the electrolyte will change. The density of the electrolyte increases with the charge

GMDSS: A User's Handbook

of the battery, due to lead ions leaving the plates and entering the electrolyte. This is measured in terms of specific gravity and maintainable batteries should be checked every month using a hydrometer. The higher the specific gravity, the greater the charge. A reading of approximately 1250 will indicate that the battery is charged, 1150 will indicate that it is discharged. A cell should not be allowed to discharge below 1180. Discharging below a specific gravity reading of 1160 will result in sulphating of the plates.

Maintenance-free batteries have acid within a gel. They cannot be opened but have a small vent on top, which should be kept clear. This type of battery is not suitable for use in areas that are susceptible to frost. Gel acid batteries will have a visual indication of charge. It will be green if charged and black if discharged.

Questions

1 What type of antenna is required to operate a Fleet F77 terminal?

2 What type of antenna is required to operate a SAT C terminal?

3 You are using your INMARSAT Fleet F77 terminal and suddenly lose your communications during an alteration of course. What might have caused this?

4 Why should you keep your whip antenna upright?

5 State the two different ways of installing a wire antenna.

6 What is the purpose of a safety loop?

7 What function does an insulator have?

8 What maintenance should you carry out on your antennae to keep them in peak condition?

9 State the safety precautions that you should observe when maintaining your antennae.

10 What tests should you carry out on your battery installation and when?

11 What are the main dangers associated with a lead acid battery?

12 State the safety precautions that should be observed when dealing with lead acid batteries.

13 Should you test the voltage of a battery when it is on load or off load?

14 What can you deduce from taking a specific gravity reading of the battery's electrolyte?

Answers

1 A large steerable parabolic antenna is required to operate a Fleet F77 terminal.

2 A small omnidirectional antenna is required to operate a SAT C terminal.

3 If you were using your INMARSAT Fleet F77 terminal and suddenly lost communications during an alteration of course, it is possible that your antenna has been put into a blind arc.

4 You should keep your whip antenna upright in order to transmit a vertically polarised signal.

5 If the radio installation is amidships, a T installation is used and if the installation is aft, an inverted L installation is used.

6 The weak link is always protected by a safety loop to ensure that the aerial does not fall to the deck and also to maintain its usability.

7 The insulators prevent the wire halyards or deck fittings from forming part of the aerial.

8 Radomes need to be kept clean to allow radio waves to pass through them. Warm soapy water should be used to remove any salt deposits, dirt or soot. All terrestrial communication antennae have insulators, which should be kept clean by washing regularly with warm soapy water. At the time of cleaning, inspect the insulators for signs of burns or damage and check all connections, earthing plates and straps.

9 It is important to ensure that the communications equipment is not capable of being used to transmit when maintenance is being carried out. Switch the antenna to ground if possible.

10 Battery voltage should be tested daily. Weekly tests should be carried out on reserve sources of energy, for example a motor generator. Monthly tests would involve a thorough inspection of the battery compartment to check the condition of the installation. Terminals should be checked for deposits, cleaned and greased. Remove the covers and ensure that the electrolyte is covering the plates. If not, top up with distilled water. Take a specific gravity reading.

11 The main dangers associated with a lead acid battery are explosion of hydrogen gas and acid burns from the electrolyte.

12 Always wear goggles and protective clothing when working with batteries. No machinery in the battery compartment should be capable of producing a spark and the area should be well ventilated at all times.

13 When testing the voltage, it should be measured off load, then when the battery is put on load you should not see a drop of more than 10%.

14 A specific gravity reading of approximately 1250 would indicate that the battery is charged, 1150 would indicate that it is discharged.

12 Maritime Safety Information

NAVTEX

A Navtex co-ordinator collates information from a national warning co-ordinator, a SAR co-ordinator and a meteorological message co-ordinator in order to prepare the Navtex service. Each of these co-ordinators, in turn, is passed information by an array of relevant bodies such as coastguards, buoyage authorities, electronic navaid providers and meteorological offices, making the resulting transmission extremely valuable to mariners. This is a fully automated service that is free of charge to owners of the relevant hardware. A GMDSS Navtex receiver contains duplication of circuitry in order to meet the IMO requirements.

The range of Navtex is usually within 300 to 400 nautical miles of the transmitting station. Exact details of the range of each individual transmitter may be found in ALRS/ADRS Volume 5. Greater ranges are possible at night because this is an MF transmission. The English language transmission is received on 518 kHz. Additional local language transmissions may be available on 490 kHz, which is the lowest frequency used in the GMDSS. Because all stations use the same frequency, each one is allocated individual time slots for transmission in order to avoid causing interference to other stations within their range. The

A Navtex receiver.

exception to this is the issue of gale warnings and SAR information, which may be broadcast at any time. Because of high atmospheric noise levels at 518 kHz, the frequency 4209.5 kHz is used to broadcast MSI in tropical and sub-tropical regions. Once set up, Navtex will work world-wide in any coastal waters offering a Navtex service without modification or additional tuning.

The Navtex unit should be programmed to display or print only messages from stations that are of interest to the user. Providing the Navtex is left switched on, with logging active, repetitions of the same message in the following 72 hours will not be printed. If the roll of thermal paper runs out in the middle of a message, the information will be stored in memory on most units providing the power is not switched off.

A complete list of Navtex stations and their single-letter designators can be found in ALRS/ADRS Volume 3 and 5 as well as in other publications.

For the purpose of Navtex, the world is divided into 21 Navareas that are identified by Roman numerals:

I (1) United Kingdom	VIII (8) India	XV (15) Chile
II (2) France	IX (9) Pakistan	XVI (16) Peru
III (3) Spain	X (10) Australia	XVII (17) Canada
IV (4) USA (east)	XI (11) Japan	XVIII (18) Canada
V (5) Brazil	XII (12) USA (west)	XIX (19) Norway
VI (6) Argentina	XIII (13) Russian Federation	XX (20) Russian Federation
VII (7) South Africa	XIV (14) New Zealand	XXI (21) Russian Federation

In addition, each Navarea is divided into A–Z coastal areas (see Figure 26). Within each Navarea there is a selection of transmitting stations that can be chosen. The transmitting stations are used when programming the Navtex receiver. Where there are no Navtex facilities, coastal areas are used when programming for EGC SafetyNET messages. A prime example of this is around Australia.

FIG 26 Worldwide Navareas for Navtex.

MESSAGE TYPES

Having programmed the stations, the next task is to decide on the types of messages that are required. Each message type may be either selected or deselected. However, because of their importance, messages A, B and D cannot be deselected and message L should not be deselected.

A Navigational warnings

B Meteorological warnings

C Ice reports

D Search and Rescue information and pirate attack warnings

E Meteorological forecasts

F Pilot service messages

G AIS messages

H LORAN messages

I Spare

J SATNAV messages

K Other electronic navaid messages

L Navigational warnings in addition to **A**

V Special services – trial allocation

W Special services – trial allocation

X Special services – trial allocation

Y Special services – trial allocation

Z No messages on hand

UK Navtex stations are using V to expand navigational warning information that has been announced under A.

An example of a printout can be seen in Figure 27. The Navtex message has a code, which in this example is EA55. The first letter of the code is the station identification – in this case E is Niton Radio. The second letter is the message type, with A being a navigational warning. The last two digits are the serial number allocated by the station and will always be between 01 and 99. WZ 1061 is a navigational warning code.

There may be a test facility on the unit which candidates should be able to operate. The resultant printout should show that all the characters have been correctly printed and a pass is indicated against each individual test. This does not test the condition of the antenna. If the equipment fails a test, there could be advice in the operator's manual but it is probable that the unit will have to be returned for repair.

An alarm will sound for priority messages. If the Navtex uses paper it will have a visible indication when it is about to run out. To reinsert a new roll, it is advisable to cut the end into a V shape as the task can be awkward. Ensure that

```
NAVTEX MESSAGE                                          EA55
WZ 1061
ENGLAND SOUTH COAST, ISLE OF WIGHT
ST CATHERINE'S POINT LIGHT 50-35N 001-18W
FIXED RED SECTOR LIGHT UNRELIABLE.
```

FIG 27 An example of a Navtex navigational warning.

the shiny side is uppermost, as this is thermal paper. Once in place, the paper should be advanced by use of the paper feed control. Do not pull the paper through as this can damage the printing head.

FEC

Forward Error Correction is a mode of telex working used by Navtex. This is the broadcast mode, sending a transmission from one station to be received by many. The whole message is sent twice. There are, therefore, only two chances to acquire the correct character. If the character is corrupted the second time, the unit will print a star or a question mark, depending on the equipment design. The second message is sent slightly behind, but mixed within, the first message. Incoming information will be held in a small memory until it has been received a second time and checked for error.

ENHANCED GROUP CALLING (EGC)

EGC enables information providers that are authorised by IMO to broadcast MSI messages, via LESs and NCSs, to ships fitted with an EGC receiver. SafetyNET is used to distribute meteorological, navigational and search and rescue messages as well as INMARSAT system messages. SafetyNET is the satellite equivalent of the terrestrial Navtex and is also a free service. To receive scheduled navigational warnings for a particular area, the terminal must be logged in to the correct ocean region NCS. When an area is covered by more than one ocean region, only one may be nominated to broadcast the information. Reception is automatic, but the terminal must be programmed with the vessel's current position and the Navarea (not individual stations) and message types that are required. Coastal areas are used around Australia, Brazil and a few other areas where there is no Navtex service. Details are available in ALRS/ADRS Volume 5.

The EGC receiver will monitor the NCS common signalling channel that will be used to send EGC messages. Important unscheduled messages are repeated six minutes after the first broadcast to increase the chance of reception. If a station wishes to be able to receive EGC messages at all times, an independent receiver is required.

EGC is most commonly associated with a SAT C terminal. Three types of EGC receiver exist. Class zero is a stand alone receiver. Class two shares a receiver with the communications terminal and will receive EGC messages when communications are not in progress. Class three has two receivers, allowing both of the above operations to take place simultaneously. If the EGC receiver is shared by the SAT C terminal, switching to exclusive EGC mode before a scheduled broadcast will ensure reception of the messages. It is important to switch it back after reception to allow resumption of routine communications.

SAT C terminals will allow the operator to request additional Navareas other than the one that the vessel is in, providing they are covered by the same ocean region. If messages are required for the North Sea, which is Navarea 1, ALRS/ADRS Volume 5 will advise that this information is available through the Atlantic Ocean Region East satellite at 1730 UTC. For example, if AORW was being used for routine communications, the operator would have to remember to log in to AORE in order to receive the SafetyNET transmission at the appropriate time. Unscheduled broadcasts of SAR information and severe weather warnings will be broadcast on all satellites that serve the area concerned. The advantage of this system over Navtex is that it can be used anywhere within satellite coverage and not just within coastal range of a Navtex transmitter.

Many SAT C terminals are manufactured with an integral GPS. Alternatively, the position can be updated automatically from the ship's position fixing system. However if either method fails, the position should be updated preferably every four hours, for safety reasons, but at least every 12 hours. After 12 hours, the EGC receiver will assume position information to be lost and print all messages higher than routine for the whole of the ocean region. Operators should print or clear the EGC log regularly to avoid filling the memory.

Questions

1 On which frequency is the English language Navtex broadcast?

2 What is the approximate range of a Navtex transmission?

3 Why is it important to program the Navtex receiver?

4 Which message types cannot be deselected?

5 What should be checked during your daily tests on the Navtex receiver?

6 What does EGC stand for?

7 What is an EGC SafetyNET message?

8 If your SAT C terminal is not interfaced with a position fixing system, how often should you update the position information?

Answers

1 The English language Navtex messages are broadcast on 518 kHz.

2 The approximate range of a Navtex transmission is 300 to 400 nautical miles, although greater ranges are possible at night.

3 It is important to program the Navtex receiver in order to prevent the printing of messages from stations outside of your area.

4 Message types A, B and D cannot be deselected. L should not be deselected.

A Navigational warnings

B Meteorological warnings

D Search and Rescue information and pirate attack warnings

L Navigational warnings in addition to A

5 The Navtex receiver should be checked for an adequate supply of paper during the daily tests.

6 EGC stands for Enhanced Group Calling.

7 An EGC SafetyNET message is the satellite equivalent of a Navtex message. Messages concerning meteorology, navigation and SAR will be included.

8 If your SAT C terminal is not interfaced with a position fixing system, you should update the position information at least every four hours for safety reasons.

13 Quick Reference Guide

FREQUENCIES AND THEIR USES

Ch 16	VHF, radiotelephony, distress, urgency, safety and calling.
Ch 06	VHF, radiotelephony, primary intership plus search and rescue.
Ch 08	VHF, radiotelephony, secondary intership.
Ch 13	VHF, radiotelephony, bridge to bridge safety of navigation.
Ch 15 and 17	VHF, radiotelephony, on board communications.
Ch 67	VHF, radiotelephony, UK small craft safety.
Ch 70	VHF, DSC, distress alerting, urgency, safety and routine calling.
490 kHz	MF, Navtex, MSI, second language frequency.
518 kHz	MF, Navtex, MSI in English.
2048 kHz	MF, radiotelephony and intership working.
2174.5 kHz	MF, telex, distress, urgency and safety.
2177 kHz	MF, DSC, ship to ship and shore to ship routine calling.
2182 kHz	MF, radiotelephony, distress, urgency, safety and calling.
2187.5 kHz	MF, DSC, distress alerting, urgency and safety calling.
2189.5 kHz	MF, DSC, international routine calling from ship to coast station.
3023 kHz	MF, radiotelephony, aeronautical search and rescue.
8291 kHz	HF, radiotelephony, distress, urgency and safety.
8414.5 kHz	HF, DSC, distress alerting, urgency and safety calling.
121.5 MHz	Homing signal from some EPIRBs.
406 MHz	COSPAS/SARSAT EPIRB.
1.5/1.6 GHz	INMARSAT
9 GHz	SART.

SIGNALS

The distress signal is a single MAYDAY

The urgency signal is a single PAN PAN

The safety signal is a single SÉCURITÉ

DSC PRIORITIES OR CALL CATEGORIES

DISTRESS

DISTRESS RELAY

URGENCY

SAFETY

EXAMPLE OF A DISTRESS CALL BY RADIOTELEPHONY

MAYDAY x 3

THIS IS

NAME x 3

CALLSIGN x 1

MMSI x 1

EXAMPLE OF AN URGENCY CALL BY RADIOTELEPHONY

PAN PAN x 3

ALL STATIONS (or an individual station) x 3

THIS IS

NAME x 3

CALLSIGN x 1

MMSI x 1

EXAMPLE OF A SAFETY CALL BY RADIOTELEPHONY ON THE WORKING CHANNEL OR FREQUENCY

SÉCURITÉ x 3

ALL STATIONS (or an individual station) x 3

THIS IS

NAME x 3

CALLSIGN x 1

MMSI x 1

EXAMPLE OF A DISTRESS MESSAGE – RADIOTELEPHONY AND INMARSAT

M MAYDAY

I IDENTIFICATION - NAME, CALLSIGN AND NUMBER

P POSITION

N NATURE OF THE DISTRESS

A ASSISTANCE REQUIRED

N NUMBER ON BOARD

O OTHER INFORMATION

O OVER

PROCEDURAL WORDS USED DURING DISTRESS WORKING

By radiotelephony:

SEELONCE MAYDAY used by controlling stations to impose radio silence.

SEELONCE FEENEE used to end radio silence and resume normal working.

THE PHONETIC ALPHABET

Alpha	**B**ravo	**C**harlie	**D**elta	**E**cho	**F**oxtrot
Golf	**H**otel	**I**ndia	**J**uliet	**K**ilo	**L**ima
Mike	**N**ovember	**O**scar	**P**apa	**Q**uebec	**R**omeo
Sierra	**T**ango	**U**niform	**V**ictor	**W**hiskey	**X**-Ray
Yankee	**Z**ulu				

INMARSAT CODES

00 AUTOMATIC DIALLING

32 MEDICAL ADVICE

38 MEDICAL ASSISTANCE OR MEDICAL EVACUATION

39 MARITIME ASSISTANCE

41 METEOROLOGICAL OBSERVATIONS

42 NAVIGATIONAL HAZARD REPORTS

43 AMVER SHIP POSITION REPORTS

Index

A3E 20
acknowledgement of distress by:
    DSC – HF 51
    DSC – MF or VHF 50
    Radiotelephony 61
Admiralty List of Radio Signals
    (ALRS) 35
AF gain control 38
AIS-SART 103
alphabet, phonetic 39, 125
antenna 107
ATU 109
Automatic Gain Control (AGC) 39
avoiding interference 40
azimuth 84

bandwidth 21, 110
batteries 111
blind arc 84
bridge to bridge communications 36

carrier 20
channel 70 36
channel uses 36
clarifier 22, 39
common signalling channel 93
control of communications 40
COSPAS/SARSAT 97

definitions:
    distress 59
    safety 65
    urgency 64
designated distress alert 48, 92
difficulty with communications 41
Digital Selective Calling (DSC) 45
direct wave 27
distress (definition) 59
distress alert by:
    DSC 47
    INMARSAT C 92

distress priority connection by:
    INMARSAT Fleet F77 86, 89
distress alert relay 51
distress call 60, 124
distress frequencies 47
distress message by
    INMARSAT C 92
    INMARSAT Fleet F77 89
    Radiotelephony 59, 124
distress signal 60, 124
documents 34
doppler 98
dual watch 38
duplex 35

electromagnetic waves 23, 107
elevation 84
Emergency Position Indicating Radio
    Beacon (EPIRB) 97
Enhanced Group Calling (EGC) 119
equipment requirements 14

F1B 22
false alerts 54, 55, 86, 104
FEC 119
float-free 99, 101
footprint 81
frequency 21, 28
frequency uses 28, 123

General Operator's Certificate 17
geostationary 81, 98
ground wave 25

H3E 21
High Frequency (HF) 24
homing 98, 101
hydrometer 112

identification of stations 31
INMARSAT C 83, 92

INMARSAT Fleet F77 83, 89
insulators 109
intership communications 36, 40
ionosphere 24
ITU publications 35

J2B 22
J3E 21

Land Earth Station (LES) 81
licensing 31
line of sight 27
Local User Terminal (LUT) 98
Long Range Certificate 18
logging in 85, 120
logging out 85, 94

maintenance of:
    antennae 110
    batteries 111
maritime access code 84, 92
Maritime Identification Digits (MID) 32
Maritime Mobile Service Identity
    (MMSI) 32
Maritime Rescue Co-ordination Centre
    (MRCC) 11
Maritime Safety Information (MSI) 115
Mayday relay call 63
Mayday relay message 63
medical advice/assistance 85, 90
Medium Frequency (MF) 23
modes of emission 20, 39
modulation 20

Navarea 116, 117
Navtex 115
Network Co-ordination Station (NCS)
    83, 85

ocean regions 82
omnidirectional antenna 23, 83, 110
on board communications 37
on scene communications 62
on scene co-ordinator 63

parabolic antenna 110
phonetic alphabet 39, 125
port operations 37
press to talk 20, 35
priorities:
    DSC 53
    INMARSAT 89
propagation 23, 24, 26, 27
public correspondence 37

R3E 22
radio check 34
radio log 73
radio wave 23
range 25, 26, 45, 101
Restricted Operator's Certificate 19
RF gain control 39
routine calling by:
    DSC 66
    INMARSAT 92
    Radiotelephony 40

safety (definition) 65
safety call 65, 123
safety connection by INMARSAT 91
safety message by:
    INMARSAT 94
    Radiotelephony 65
SafetyNET 83, 119
safety signal 65, 123
SART 100
sea areas 13
seelonce feenee 62, 125
seelonce mayday 62, 125
semi-duplex 36
signals 124
simplex 35
single sideband 21
sky wave 26
space wave 27
specific gravity 112
squelch 38
STCW 19
store and forward 83

tests; daily, weekly and monthly 34
test transmissions 34
time division multiplexing 83
transceiver 38
transmitter power 38, 39
transportable VHF 107
tuning 109
two-digit INMARSAT codes 85, 125

undesignated distress alert 48, 92
Universal Time, Co-ordinated (UTC) 34
urgency (definition) 64
urgency call 65, 124
urgency connection by INMARSAT 90

urgency message by:
    INMARSAT 90
    Radiotelephony 64
urgency signal 64

Very High Frequency (VHF) 23
voltage 112
volume control 38

watch keeping 33
wavelength 23
weak link 109
whip antenna 109
wire aerial 109
working channel/frequency 36

Tip

Exam candidates may find the AMERC online GMDSS quiz helpful: www.amerc.ac.uk/quiz